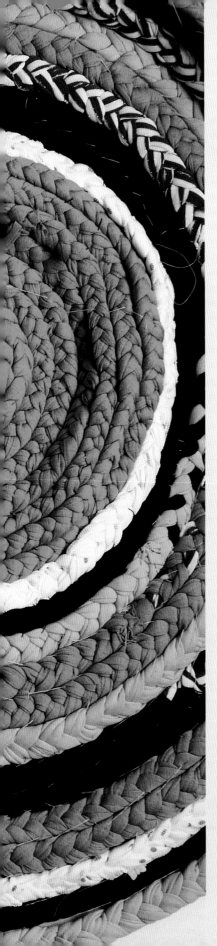

HOME

BECI ORPIN

hardie grant books
MELBOURNE · LONDON

CONTENTS

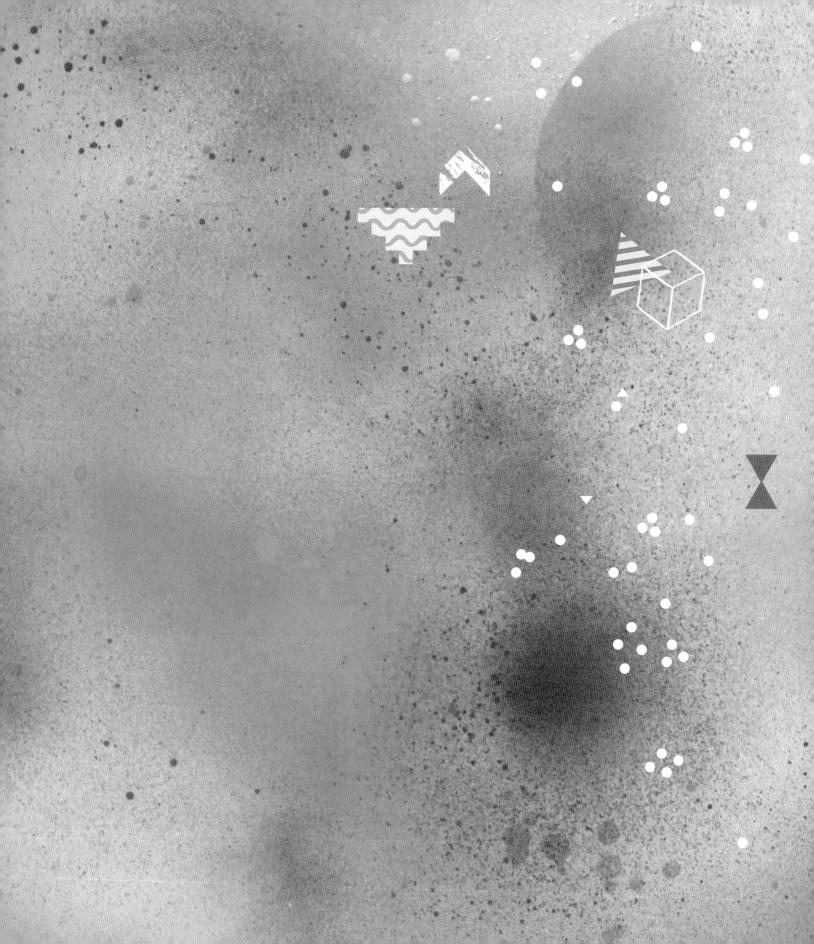

For Raph, Tyke and Ari — you are the best thing for turning my house into a home.

INTRODUCTION

AS YOU CAN TELL BY THE TITLE, THIS BOOK IS ALL ABOUT 'HOME'.

▶

Here you will find some fun projects for nice things to make for your house, as well as some inspiring images of some my favourite spaces.

While I was making this book, it got me thinking about the things that really make a house a home (as the old cliché goes). For me, it needs all (or at the very least some) of the following: lots of cushions, piles of books, artwork on the walls, flowers in vases, two cats, collections of much-loved objects and the smell of something cooking. And most importantly: family is number one on the list of what makes my house a home!

Like the voyeur in most of us, I love looking in other people's houses. Sometimes I take this voyeurism to a slightly stalker-ish level. I love to go for a ride around the streets in my neighbourhood on warm evenings, when people leave their doors and windows open. You can smell the food they are cooking, hear snippets of conversations and sometimes get a sneak peek inside too. (Sorry if you live in my 'hood. I promise I would never take the voyeurism any further than that!) All these people with their own houses, making them the way they like. I find this both intriguing and comforting.

But taking an interest in other people's spaces doesn't have to be quite so stalker-ish. These days there are umpteen blogs, websites, books and magazines that focus on the idea of 'house tours'. Throughout these pages you will find photos I've taken of my friends' houses (or in some cases photos they have taken). I encouraged them all to *not* clean up, so the spaces could be captured in their everyday state. To me, seeing a friend's house in its 'natural state' is often more inspiring than looking at styled interiors in a magazine.

More often than not, the homes I like the most are not the ones that are über clean and styled to the hilt. It's the ones with the slightly threadbare couch covered by an old blanket, where the pictures on the wall hang a little bit crooked and the coat rack is slightly overflowing. I'm guessing this is because this is what my house is like. Not at all perfect, but lived in and, above all, well loved.

So here is my version of what a home is. Most likely it is different to yours, but I hope you will find some of the images and projects inside inspiring, and find some ways to make your house more of a home.

LIVING SPACES

OH, LIVING ROOM. HOW I WISH I GOT TO SPEND MORE TIME IN YOU. FILLED WITH CUSHIONS AND RUGS AND COMFORTABLE CHAIRS, YOU ARE THE CENTRE OF RELAXATION IN A HOME.

When we first moved into our house, we used our lounge room as a second office for Raph. We thought we could squeeze all of our relaxation needs into a tiny windowless space joined to our kitchen. But as our kids got physically bigger, we saw how wrong we were. We quickly came to the conclusion that a bigger lounge room was more important than a second office.

The thought of decorating a whole new room had me delirious with excitement (I literally didn't sleep for one whole night) and, when we had the finished product…Oh, how I relished it. What a huge difference it made to the way we used our house. We now had a separate place for Sunday afternoon snoozes; for watching a DVD; for cubby-house creations; for displaying our favourite objects. It's become our favourite space in the house. Truly a room for us to 'live' in.

I like to see how other people create living spaces: the furniture they choose, how they use artworks and colour, how they put their treasured possessions together on shelves, even the mess they allow to be seen. It all comes together in a personal way, and irrespective of budget (often there is very little), it usually still turns out to be a beautiful space, and above all, a wonderful reflection of the individual that lives there.

My favourite thing about living rooms: the curation of objects and books you often find in them. If you look closely you can often get a mini insight into the psyche of the owner via the things on their shelves and walls. Luckily, my friends all have lovely psyches, and shelves.

LIVING
SPACES
PROJECTS

In the following pages you will find some projects to add some loveliness to your living space. I've tried to incorporate all the things that I think make a living

room extra nice, such as wall art, shelving, plants and even a house for a small animal. Go forth and make pretty!

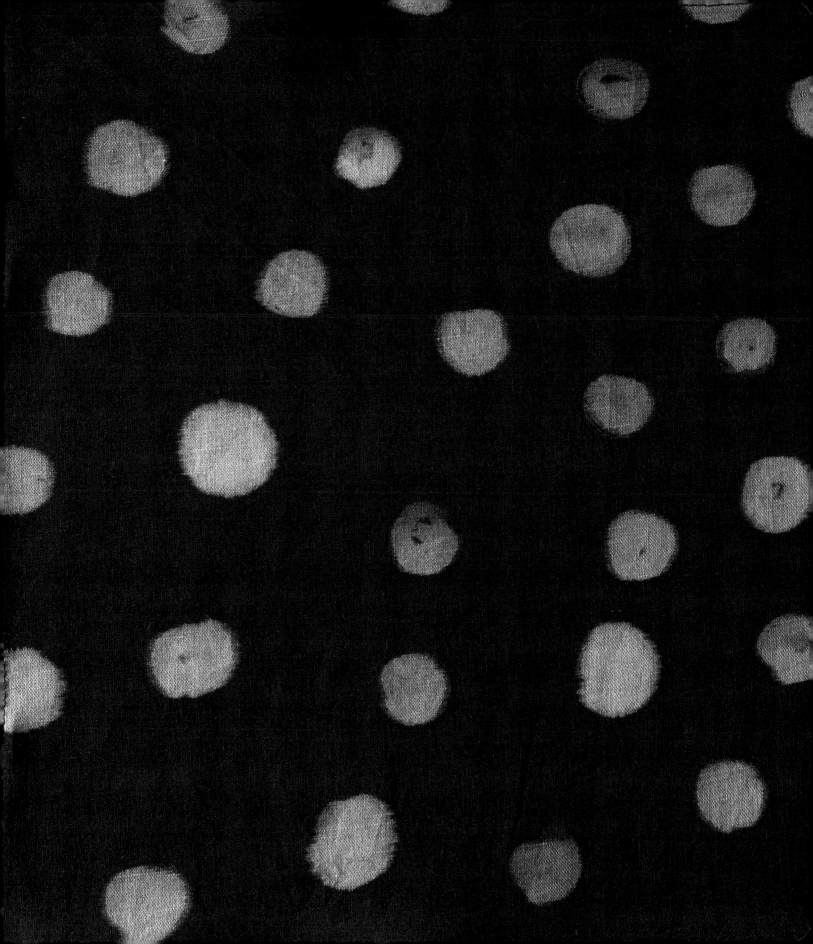

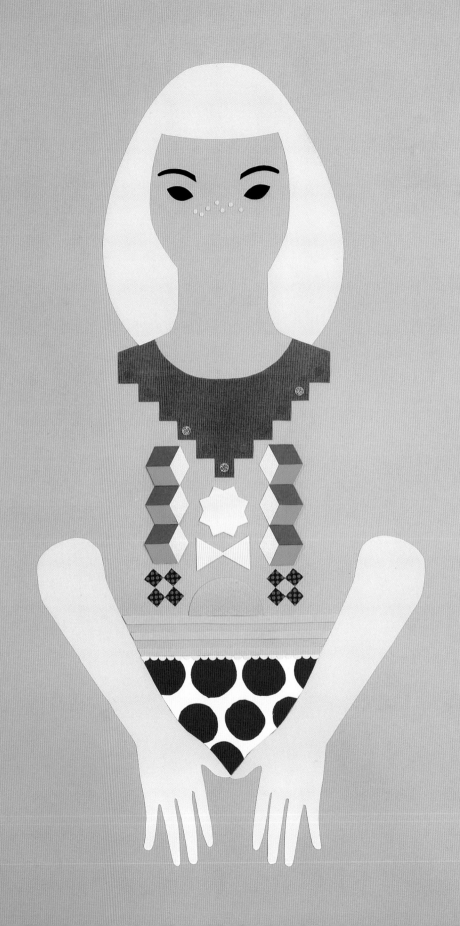

PAPER PATCHWORK

I come from a long line of patchworkers – okay, maybe 'long line' is a bit of a stretch, but my granny and my auntie made quilts. I still have the 'crazy' quilts my granny made for me and my sister when we were little. They are made from beautiful scraps of fabrics from the sixties and seventies, and are some of my most treasured possessions. Although I have designed a few quilts, I'm yet to delve into actually sewing one myself. It is high on my bucket list, though.

Patchwork has also been a common theme in my work and I reference it often: I love the use of repeats and simple shapes, and then putting pattern inside those shapes, which is where the idea for this project came from. It is an inexpensive way to make a nice piece of wall art for a room, and it is a lot easier and quicker than a fabric patchwork.

YOU WILL NEED

◦ Paper Patchwork templates (page 209)

◦ coloured card (I've used mustard, navy, pale pink and aqua)

◦ craft knife or scissors

◦ ruler and cutting mat

◦ Blu-tack or repositionable adhesive dots to stick to the wall

Difficulty: Easy

HERE WE GO

1

Cut out all pieces using the templates. This pattern fits together best when the edges are straight, so use a ruler when cutting.

3

Note: the aqua pieces are made up of a smaller triangle and a bigger triangle.

2

Sort all your pieces into stacks by size and colour (it can get confusing otherwise).

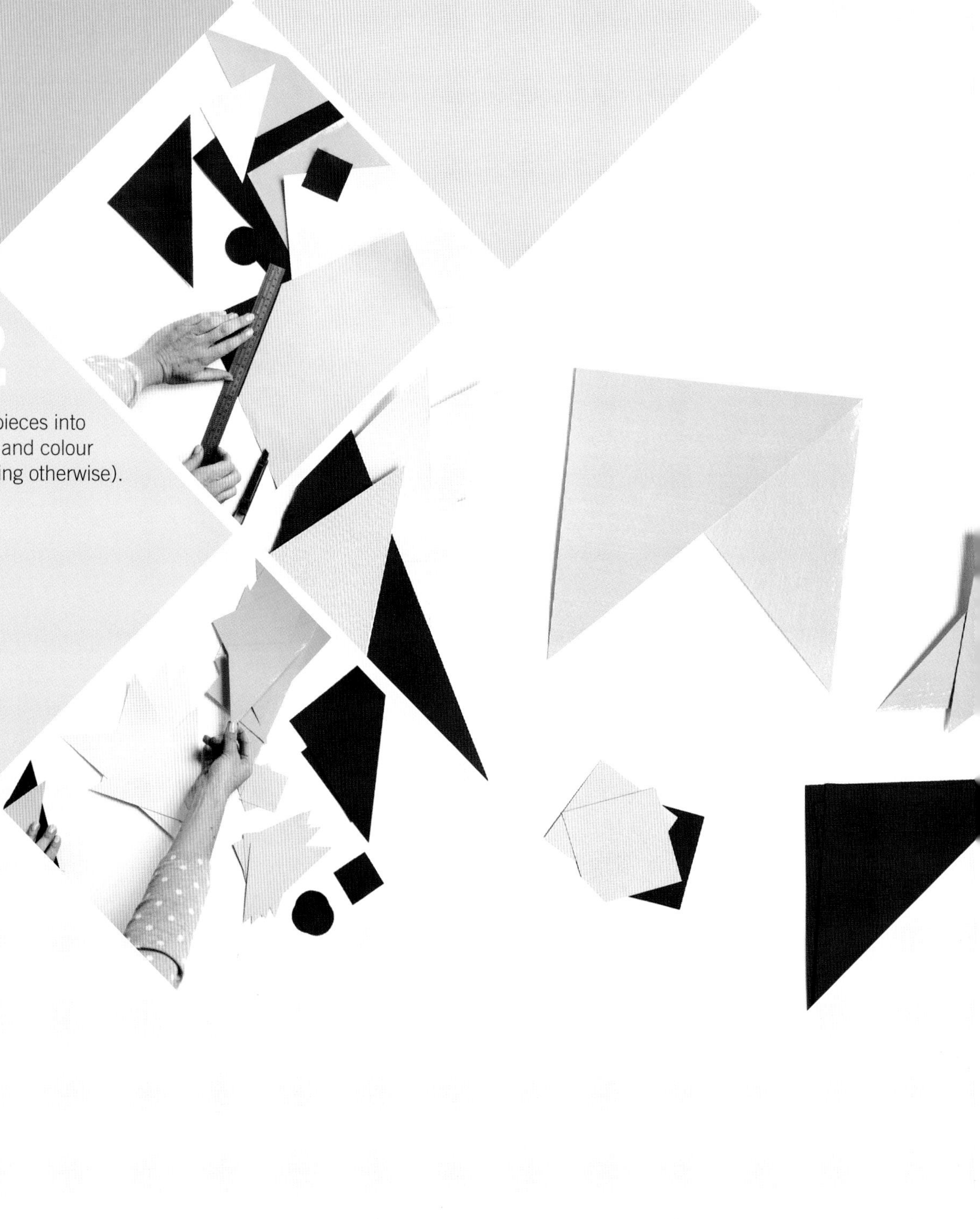

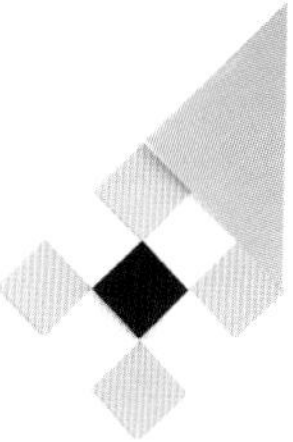

4

Assemble the pieces on the wall. Start from the centre and work outwards to the right and left, making sure you are keeping the lines straight as you go.

tip

If you can't find card in the exact colour you are after, buy white card and paint it. This also adds a nice texture.

5

Complete the patchwork by working outwards to the top and bottom. It might take a few adjustments to get all of the pieces sitting together right!

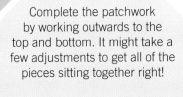

BOX SHELVES

It is often said that one can never have enough storage. This is very true in my house. Although I love our home's 120-year-old heritage, the Victorian era was not known for its built-in cupboards. This, combined with my penchant for collecting, means that new storage solutions are often required. These shelves do require some proper tools and the hammering in of nails; however, the end result – a sweet place to put your treasured items – is very much worth it.

Triangle shelf:
◦ three 35 cm (13¾ in) long pieces of 19 x 70 mm (¾ x 2¾ in) timber, cut with a mitre saw at a 30-degree angle at each end. (This is a hard ask, I know, but many hardware stores will cut timber for you.) ◦ drill and 6 mm (¼ in) drill bit ◦ short length of 6 mm (¼ in) rope or cord

Rectangle shelf:
◦ two 25 cm (9¾ in) and two 45 cm (17¾ in) long pieces of 19 x 70 mm (¾ x 2¾ in) timber, cut with a mitre saw at a 45-degree angle at each end ◦ 2 m (79 in) of 6 mm (¼ in) rope or cord ◦ 40 mm (1½ in) wooden bead

Square shelf:
◦ 40 cm (15¾ in) square of 3 mm (⅛ in) plywood ◦ four 40 cm (15¾ in) pieces of 19 x 70 mm (¾ x 2¾ in) timber, cut with a mitre saw at a 45-degree angle at each end ◦ Box Shelf template (page 206) ◦ pencil, acrylic paint and paintbrush ◦ picture wire

For all shelves:
◦ construction adhesive (such as Liquid Nails) ◦ hammer and small nails ◦ fine grit sandpaper

Difficulty: Hard

1

Triangle shelf:
sand any rough edges and lay the pieces of timber out in a triangle shape.

HERE WE GO

3

Spread construction adhesive on the ends of each piece of timber, on the mitred edge and also on the flat side of the piece it will join to. Allow to dry for around 5 minutes, depending on the glue you use. This will allow the glue to stick better. Stick the pieces together to form a triangle. Allow to dry overnight.

2

Drill a hole approximately 10 cm (4 in) from the top point of the triangle on the two side pieces.

Use sandpaper to sand off any dried adhesive.

5

Hammer a small nail into each corner for extra strength. Cover up the holes using small amounts of adhesive.

6

Thread the ends of the rope through the holes from the outside and knot inside the triangle.

Rectangle shelf:
sand any rough edges and
lay the pieces of timber out in a
rectangle shape.
Repeat steps 3 to 5 to assemble the rectangle.
Once completed, place rope around outside.
Secure with a wooden bead and a tied
knot (you might want to tie a few
knots to make it really secure.

9

Once the paint is dry,
nail the plywood back to the
square shelf.

Square shelf:
assemble the square shelf
as you did the rectangle. Trace
out the template in a repeat pattern on
the plywood square. Paint the pattern. (You
might like to use masking tape to get straight
edges, although I prefer more of an
organic look.)

10

Add an extra two nails
one-third of the way down
from the top edge and attach
some wire to hang it from. If you would
like the shelves to hang flat you could add a
hook on top instead.

COLOUR BLOCKED CHAIRS

A beautifully designed chair is definitely a weakness
for me. Over the years I have acquired more than a few:
some from expensive shops, some from the side of the road. This
weakness may have recently become a little out of hand … I now have
more chairs than we can comfortably fit in the house. In our shed there is a little
chair 'waiting place', where – among other things – there are currently three sets of
dining chairs (that means we own four sets including the ones we are actually using around
the dining table). See what I mean by the 'out of hand' bit? Anyway, now I've put a stop to it. No
more buying (for a while anyway), so let's do a bit of 'upcycling' instead. Which is where this project
comes into play. Here is a way you can make your old chairs look great. I actually tracked these ones down
specifically for this project; they cost me $10 each from a local oppy (score!), and I have seen others similar
for even cheaper.

YOU WILL NEED

◦ wooden chair or chairs

◦ coarse-grade sandpaper

◦ paintbrushes: one wide and one for details

◦ masking tape

◦ paint (I used acrylic interior paint: the
small sample pots are cheap and
good for projects like this)

◦ clear varnish

Difficulty:
Medium

1

Sketch out some ideas of which colours you would like to go on each part of the chair. Consider each part of the chair separately: seat, legs, top, back support and so on. Also consider basic patterns as well as just block colour.

HERE WE GO

3

Consider the order you will paint in and use masking tape to protect any areas of the chair and to get clean lines.

2

If your chair has varnish or paint (most secondhand chairs will) use the sandpaper to rub off the varnish on the areas you are going to paint.

4

You might need to paint a few coats (I used three on these ones). Wait until one area is completely dry before painting the next.

tip

Try to choose a varnish that matches the existing varnish on the chair (for example, matte, satin or gloss finish).

5

Once all the painting is complete, varnish the painted areas: this will give them more longevity.

ROPE BASKETS

These baskets have made quite a regular appearance
in the craft realm lately. It's no wonder: they contain all the
right things for a perfect project. Cheap to make, addictive to work
on and the end result is very boast-worthy. AND they are useful and have
an awesome ethnic vibe (which I'm pretty fond of) too.
The hardest choice for these baskets was colours. I thought finding nice cord would be
tricky, but with just one trip to my local craft megastore I was overwhelmed by choice! Sailing
and marine shops are good places to look for nice rope as well.

YOU WILL NEED

◦ cord or rope: the amount will vary depending on how big you want your basket and the thickness of the rope.
(The biggest basket shown here used 10 metres or 11 yards of rope.)

◦ thick embroidery thread, cut into manageable lengths (1–2 metres or yards)

◦ wool needle with a big eye (I found the plastic ones were easiest to use)

◦ pins

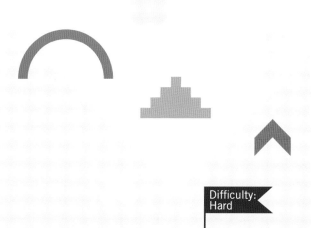

Difficulty:
Hard

Wrap the thread around the end of the rope a few times. Wrap the thread tightly: close together at first, then with a little space between the wraps.

3

Wrap the thread where the loop finishes and tie a knot.

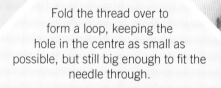
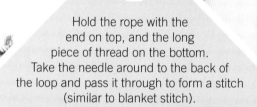

Fold the thread over to form a loop, keeping the hole in the centre as small as possible, but still big enough to fit the needle through.

4

Hold the rope with the end on top, and the long piece of thread on the bottom. Take the needle around to the back of the loop and pass it through to form a stitch (similar to blanket stitch).

Continue to stitch as
you wrap the rope around.
Stitches should be close together
at the base of the basket, then start to
spread out a bit more.

6

Once you are happy with
the base, start pinning the
rope vertically before stitching.
This will help to build a good shape.

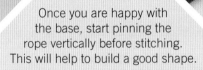

tip

You could also paint or dye
the rope to give a different effect.

When you run out of
thread, knot a new piece to
the end of the old piece. You can
then tuck the knot between the rounds
of rope.

8

To finish, complete the
final stitch, tie a knot and
weave the thread into the row of
rope below before cutting.

SILVER THREAD
LOOKS CUTE WITH
ALL COLOURS!

STAMPED WALL DECOR

After studying textile design, pattern has became one of my great loves. Wallpaper in particular. As yet we have no wallpapered walls in our house, although I am determined to paper our staircase one day. I even ordered some wallpaper samples, and they were stuck on the staircase wall for months on end, while we considered and considered. We are still yet to take the plunge. This wall decoration is much easier and cheaper to put on to your wall than designer rolls. Plus it involves making stamps, which is super fun. Another bonus: if you change your mind and decide you don't like it, you can simply paint over it.

YOU WILL NEED

◦ blank stamp and stamp-cutting tools

◦ Wall Decor templates (page 209)

◦ pencil and ruler or tape measure

◦ acrylic paint and small roller

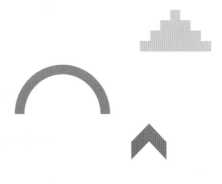

Difficulty: Medium

HERE WE GO

1

Wash the wall you plan to apply the stamp to (sugar soap is always good for washing walls). Draw the stamp design onto a blank stamp and cut.

3

Measure the wall and indictate with a pencil dot where you would like the stamps to be placed.

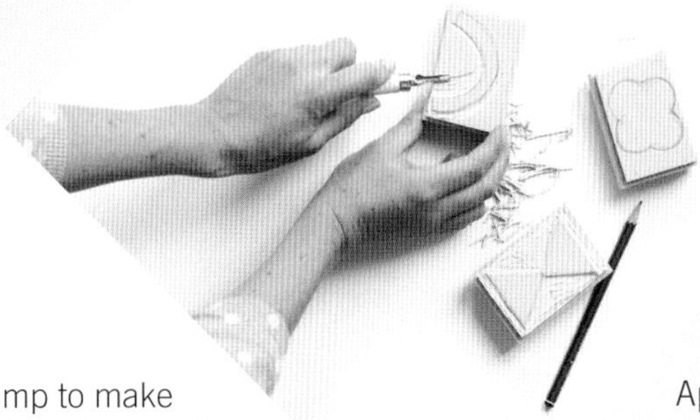

Test the stamp to make sure all areas have been cut away.

Apply paint to the stamp with a roller to ensure an even coat.

Start stamping.

FOREVER CACTUS

I talked about my love of cacti and succulents in
my first book, *Find & Keep*. My love still stands, but truth
be told, I have been known to kill the odd cactus. Even when
I've given it a nice sunny spot, a-little-but-not-too-much water, lots of
cactus friend company, and even the occasional song, sometimes they still
just die. So, here is a plant that will never die. That is because it is not a plant. It
is made from material that was once a plant, so technically … Anyway, who cares if it's
living or dead? These guys look pretty, are fun to make and will stay alive regardless of your
watering habits (they still might like a song though). For this project I used a hot-glue gun. Up until
this moment I was a HGG virgin: shocking, I know! That shiz was a CRAFT REVELATION! I encourage you
to go forth and invest in the HGG. You will not be disappointed.

YOU WILL NEED

Cacti:
◦ Cactus templates (page 210) ◦ thick card or box board ◦ craft knife and cutting mat ◦ paintbrush
and acrylic paint (we used three different greens and some olive and yellow for detailing)

Paper flowers:
◦ coloured paper for flowers, cut into strips approximately 3 cm (1¼ in)
wide x 30 cm (12 in) long. Two strips per flower.
◦ needle and thread ◦ small pompoms ◦ paper glue ◦ hot-glue
gun or PVA glue

Containers:
◦ empty, clean food tins (or other
containers, such as plant pots)
◦ small rocks or pebbles
(2–3 handfuls)
◦ newspaper or
polyester
toy fill

Difficulty:
Medium

HERE WE GO

1
Trace the cactus shapes from the templates onto the card and cut out with a craft knife. Make sure you cut out all the slots as well.

2
Paint the cut-out pieces on both sides. Make sure you paint the edge of the card and the inside of the slots too.

3
Once the paint is dry, add details, such as spots and stripes.

4

Slot the pieces together
to create the 3D cactus.

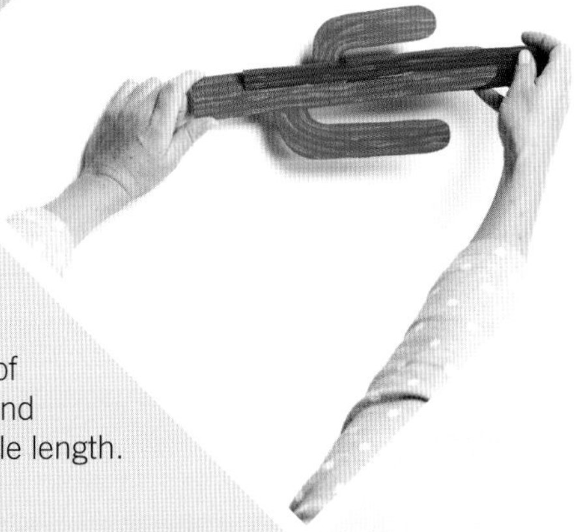

6

Add a stitch at one end
to hold the flower together.
The stitch will form the centre of
your flower.

5

Take the strips of
coloured paper and
concertina fold the whole length.

7

Using paper glue, stick both ends of the two paper strips together (this can be quite fiddly).

9

Place some rocks in the bottom of the tin (save some for the top of the tin too), and then three-quarters fill with toy fill or scrunched newspaper.

8

Using the hot-glue gun or PVA, stick the pompom to the centre of the flower, and when it is dry, stick the flower to the assembled cactus.

Add the remaining rocks and insert the cactus, so the cactus is held upright by the rocks.

KEEP YOUR EYE OUT FOR CUTE TINS AT SPECIALIST FOOD STORES

CARDBOARD HOUSE

Cardboard boxes go down a treat in our house. In the days when we used to run my clothing label, Princess Tina, dozens of boxes would turn up to pack orders into. Tyke and Ari would be in heaven. Most of the boxes went to customers, but a few ended up being converted into cars, rockets, helmets, monster-suits and so on. And, of course, what cat does not like a box? This project takes the humble box conversion to the next level. It's suitable for both small humans and small-to-medium-sized animals – neither of whom will appreciate its extra prettiness. But you will, and that is the whole point, right? I did go and buy this box especially for the project, mostly because I wanted a decent-sized box, and we only had small ones. I bought it from a self-storage place and it was super cheap (although it was a bit of a bugger getting it home on my bike). I also used extra-wide washi tape. It is not cheap, but so awesome, and has lots of uses. Masking tape or duct tape would work great, too (electrical supply stores often have duct tape in great colours!).

YOU WILL NEED

For the house:
◦ cardboard box: the one I used was a 50 cm (20 in) cube ◦ extra cardboard for the roof: I used 1400 GSM box board ◦ pencil ◦ craft knife

To decorate:
◦ 20 cm (8 in) wide washi tape (or coloured adhesive tape) ◦ white paint pen ◦ round dot stickers ◦ pompom (for door handle)

Difficulty:
Easy

HERE WE GO

Tape the box together, taking into consideration which side will be the top (don't tape this side). Tape all edges, outside and inside, if you would like your house to withstand more use.

2

Cut the front and back flaps into triangles, so the left and right side can be taped on to form part of the pitched roof. Tape the right- and left-hand side flaps to the front and back flaps to form the base of the roof.

3

Cut extra card to form the peak of the roof. If it is one big sheet, simply score down the middle, then tape in place. If you're using two separate pieces, tape them together allowing some flexibility for the peak to bend. Tape the ends of the roof piece in place too.

4

Use a pencil to draw up the doors and windows and cut them out using a craft knife. Leave one side of the door attached as a hinge.

Add an extra circle of
card for the door handle.
Pierce a hole through both
circle and door and tie on a pompom,
securing it with tape on the back of
the door.

6

Add more details and
decorations using a white
paint pen and stickers. Finish by
attaching the roof.

TRY SOME
DIFFERENT
WINDOW
SHAPES

SILHOUETTE PORTRAITS

One of the best presents I ever made was for my mum
on her 60th birthday. Like any proud mum and grandma, mine
loves a family portrait. She prefers the more informal type, taken at
home, but I still duck out of them at any opportunity! Now, especially being
a mum myself, I do understand the value of these family pics. So for her birthday,
I wanted to give my mum a family portrait, but my version.
After much thought and procrastination, I decided upon a silhouette family portrait. I have
used silhouettes a lot in my work, but I was still surprised how great it turned out. Most importantly,
my mum loved it. It's still on her wall, and even though it is just silhouettes, you can tell how much the
kids have changed since then by looking at it. Just like a photo!

YOU WILL NEED:

◦ digital camera (a phone camera is fine)

◦ printouts of photos (a home printer is okay)

◦ tracing paper, pencil and scissors

◦ coloured card for silhouettes (darker colours work best) and
coloured card for circles

◦ white card for the picture base

◦ 16 mm (⅝ in) circle cutter

◦ paper glue

◦ frame

Difficulty:
Hard

2 for
5¢

1

Choose a white wall for your subjects to pose against. Mark a space just in front of the wall for people to stand on, and also mark a spot for the photographer to stand on. (This will ensure that all the photos are the same scale.) Get everyone to stand on the spot in profile (side-on) and take a photo of each person. Make sure you have the camera at their head height so the profile is straight on.

HERE WE GO

3

Place tracing paper over the photo print and trace the outline of each person's head.

2

Print each of the photos on paper of the same size (make sure the scale is not changed).

Try using different
colours for different family
members.

4

Transfer the traced
outline onto card and cut out
the shape. Don't rush it! The more
detail and closer to the line you are
able to get, the more likeness to the
person you will achieve.

6

Using the circle cutter,
cut out circles for the border
and stick them down. Place the
whole assembly in a frame and display
it proudly.

5

Once you have all the
silhouettes cut out, arrange
them on the white background
and stick them down.

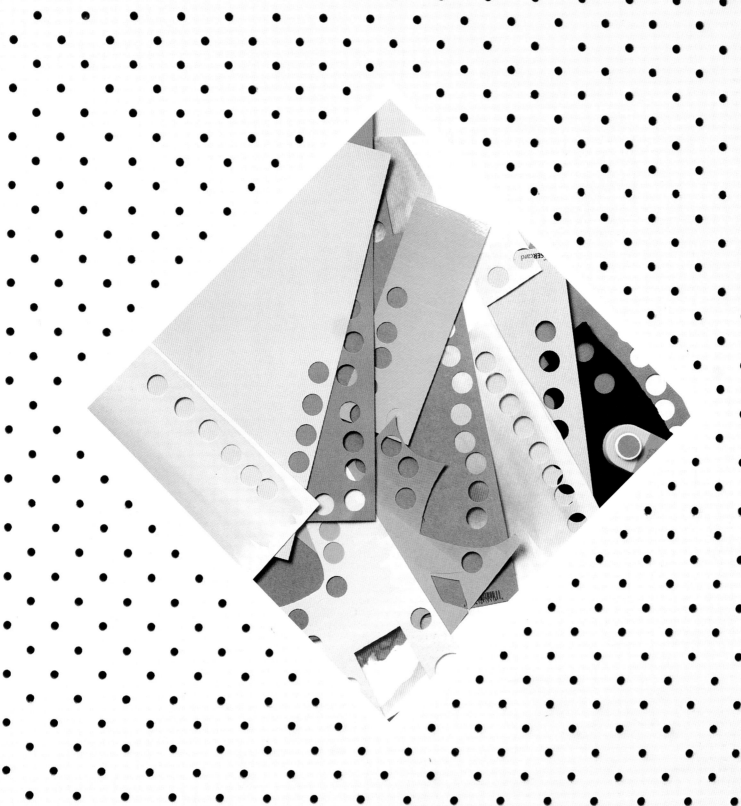

EATING SPACES

ALTHOUGH OUR KITCHEN IS MADE UP OF AWFUL LAMINATE BENCHES AND DYSFUNCTIONAL CUPBOARDS IT IS ALSO FILLED WITH OUR HAND-PICKED KITCHEN THINGS.

Countless ceramic bowls of different shapes and colours, patterned basketweave food covers we lugged back from Malaysia, my prized KitchenAid mixer. All of these things turn our kitchen from a lacklustre room devoid of personality into a room that is the heart of our home.

The kitchen is not only the heart of our home, it is also the room we spend most time in. Of course we cook and eat in it several times a day; our kitchen table is also where homework is done, where much tea (or wine) is shared with friends, where many games and family discussions are had.

Our house is semidetached, and the neighbours who share our wall are a retired Italian couple, Nina and Dom. They are the optimum neighbours, always bringing in our bins for us, handing us basil seedlings over the fence, on some occasions even mowing our lawn (without us even asking!). Every day around 3 pm we are tormented by the delicious smells of Nina's cooking. But it doesn't always end in torment. Sometimes we yell over the fence, 'Nina what are you cooking? Smells amazing!' and before long a plate is brought over to us, we sit down at our kitchen table and have a chat. That situation to me is the ultimate ideal of what kitchens should be about. Not just a place to share food, but a place to share a whole bunch more.

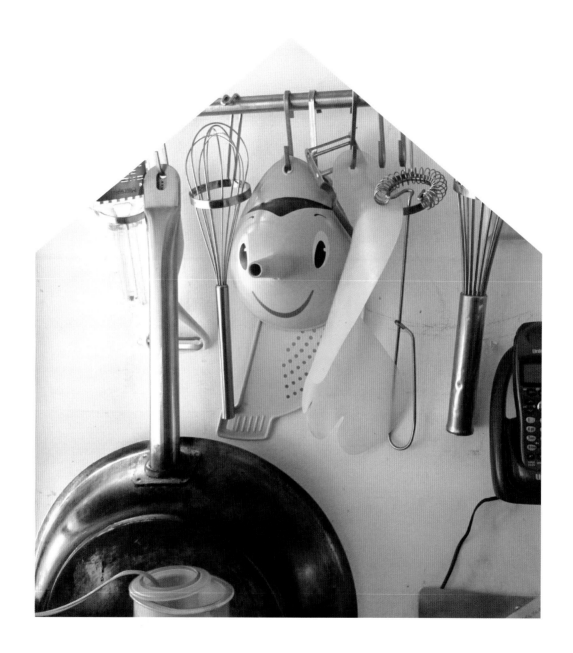

ONE OF THE NICEST PARTS OF TAKING THESE PHOTOS WAS ALL THE CUPS OF TEA I GOT TO HAVE IN FRIENDS KITCHENS. SIMPLE ACTIONS LIKE THIS ARE THE EPITOME OF 'HOME' TO ME.

EATING
SPACES
PROJECTS

Here are some projects to make for your kitchen. The best thing about these projects is that not only do they look good, they are also useful and serve a purpose: my favourite kind of project!

STORAGE JARS

I do like my house, but it is in need of a renovation. This will happen one day, but it will not happen in the immediate future. So at the moment I just have to turn a blind eye to numerous things that annoy me in my house. This is particularly hard when it comes to our kitchen. I despise our kitchen.

From the cream laminate to the complete lack of bench space, it is an advertisement for bad design and bland colour schemes. Regardless, it is still the part of our house where we spend most of our time. As a Band-Aid of sorts, I like to add some nice things to the kitchen as a distraction. And it almost works. These kitchen containers are one such thing. And they are easy and cheap to make, too. Here, rather than instructions, you will find a list of ideas for you to add to your kitchen containers. Go crazy!

YOU WILL NEED

◦ variety of glass storage jars: these can be recycled jars or ones bought new

◦ glass and porcelain markers

◦ acrylic paint and brushes, or paint pens

◦ patterned washi tape

◦ circular stickers

Difficulty:
Easy

1

Paint patterns using the glass pens: try stripes, dots of same scale, dots of different scale, triangles, stars, geometric shapes, zigzags, wiggly lines.

HERE WE GO

3

Make a polka-dot pattern using circular stickers.

2

Stick down strips of washi tape.

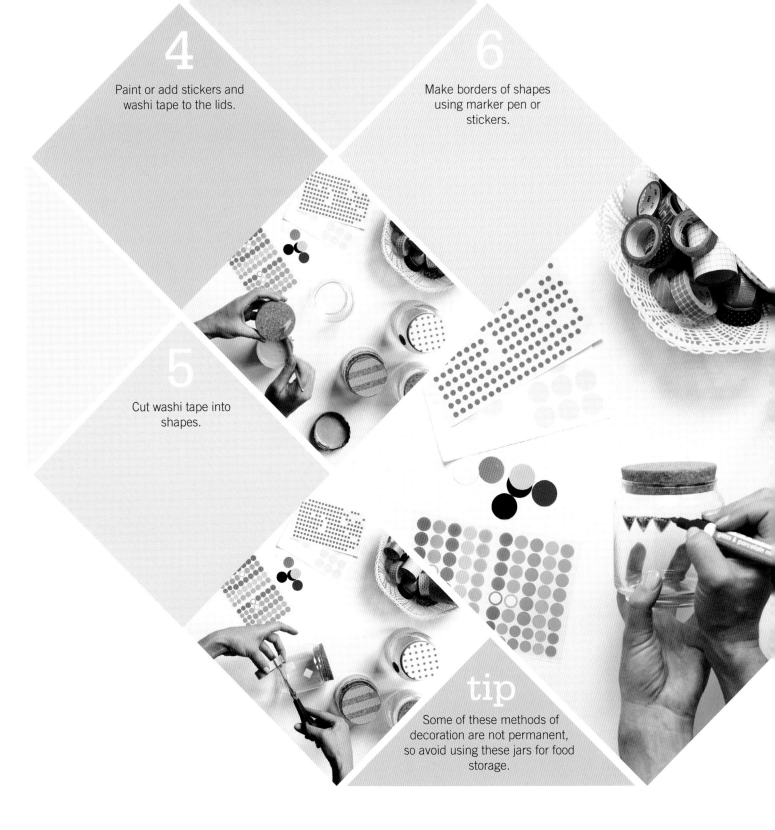

4

Paint or add stickers and washi tape to the lids.

5

Cut washi tape into shapes.

6

Make borders of shapes using marker pen or stickers.

tip

Some of these methods of decoration are not permanent, so avoid using these jars for food storage.

CHAOS
TABLECLOTH

A funny thing inspired this project. I had a tablecloth
on my list of projects I wanted to try, but wasn't sure what to
do with it. One of my studio helpers, Alice, had been dyeing some
streamers for an exhibition I was having. Alice laid the streamers to dry on
a piece of cloth, and once finished the cloth ended up in my studio … The way
the dye had bled onto the fabric was so pretty! And BAM! there it was: my tablecloth
idea! A happy accident if ever there was one. We then set about testing how to get these
accidental marks, but this time not by accident. We ended up in my backyard, with a big piece of
white fabric spread out over the grass, throwing dye around with droppers and spray bottles. It was chaos!
And so much fun too. Almost more fun than the party it would be used at.

YOU WILL NEED

◦ one white tablecloth or large piece of white fabric (a bedsheet would also be fine)

◦ red, yellow and blue dye: we used vegetable dyes, but if you would like a more
permanent effect, use regular dyes

◦ 4 spray bottles

◦ 3 eyedroppers and 3 vessels for dye

◦ backing cloth or paper to put underneath
(best not to use newspaper, because
the ink could bleed onto the white
fabric)

Difficulty:
Medium

1

Mix up the dyes so they are quite diluted and fill the spray bottles and the vessels for the eyedroppers, one for each colour. Also fill one spray bottle just with water.

3

You will need a large area for this part, and also preferably a place where it won't matter if drops of dye go flying about. Lay backing paper or cloth down, and then lay the damp fabric on top of it.

2

The effect you are after will work better on damp fabric, so wet the fabric thoroughly, and then give it a good wring out.

It is better for the fabric
to lie flat while it is drying – if
you hang it up to dry, the dyes
could run.

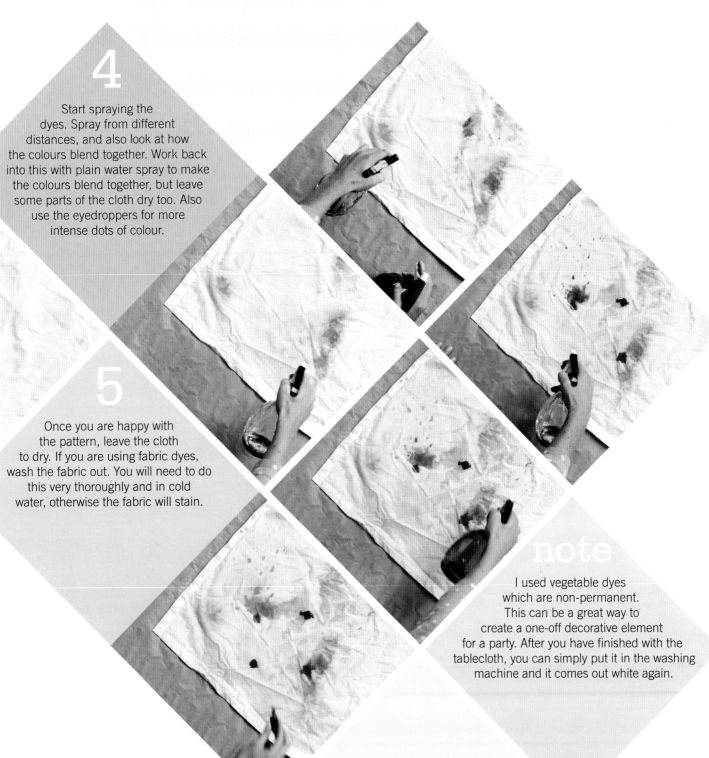

4

Start spraying the
dyes. Spray from different
distances, and also look at how
the colours blend together. Work back
into this with plain water spray to make
the colours blend together, but leave
some parts of the cloth dry too. Also
use the eyedroppers for more
intense dots of colour.

5

Once you are happy with
the pattern, leave the cloth
to dry. If you are using fabric dyes,
wash the fabric out. You will need to do
this very thoroughly and in cold
water, otherwise the fabric will stain.

note

I used vegetable dyes
which are non-permanent.
This can be a great way to
create a one-off decorative element
for a party. After you have finished with the
tablecloth, you can simply put it in the washing
machine and it comes out white again.

ONCE DRY, IRON
THE TABLECLOTH
(OR NOT!) AND GET
READY TO PARTY!

FRIDGE MAGNETS

Like most other things in our life, our fridge is
generally in a pretty chaotic state. The inside varies
between organised and overflowing, but it's the outside
that's the most crazy. It acts as our family noticeboard, photo
album, scrapbook, business-card holder, ever-changing art gallery,
takeaway-menu filing system, shopping list display, et cetera. No matter
how many times we declutter it, within a few days we are right back where we
started. So, we obviously should have a nice collection of fridge magnets to hold all this
chaos in place. Not so. Good magnets are somewhat hard to come by. Japan fed me a steady
stream for a while, but they seem to have all disappeared. Which is why I have made my own. These
little magnets seem to make all the chaos okay. You can customise them, too: put the cranky house on that
bill you really don't want to pay. Put the happy ice-cream on the awesome party invitation, and so on.

YOU WILL NEED

◦ Fridge Magnets templates (page 211)

◦ white mounting board (or any other thick card)

◦ coloured paper or thin card: navy, pink, pale pink, aqua, blue, white, gold

◦ white pastel or pencil, dark blue felt-tip marker

◦ magnets (the ones I used had adhesive backs)

◦ small scissors, paper glue, double-sided
adhesive tape and circle punch

Difficulty:
Medium

SHOPPING

MILK
RICOTTA
BUTTER
VINO
MANDARINS

Herzliche Weihnachtsgrüße

HERE WE GO

1

Cut out all the pieces using the templates.

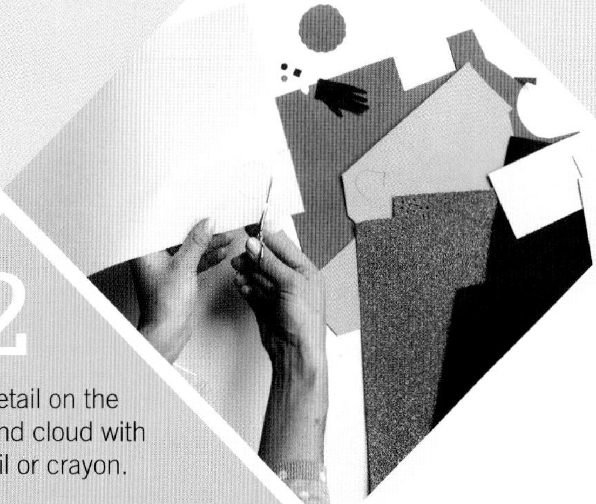

2

Add the detail on the house roof and cloud with white pencil or crayon.

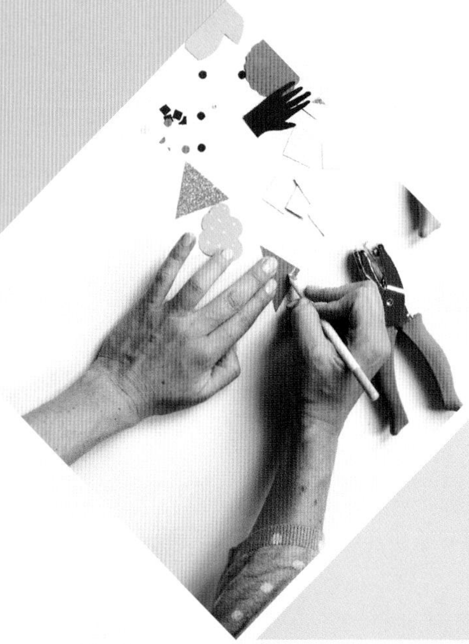

3

Add eyes with felt-tip marker to the flower lady and happy ice-cream.

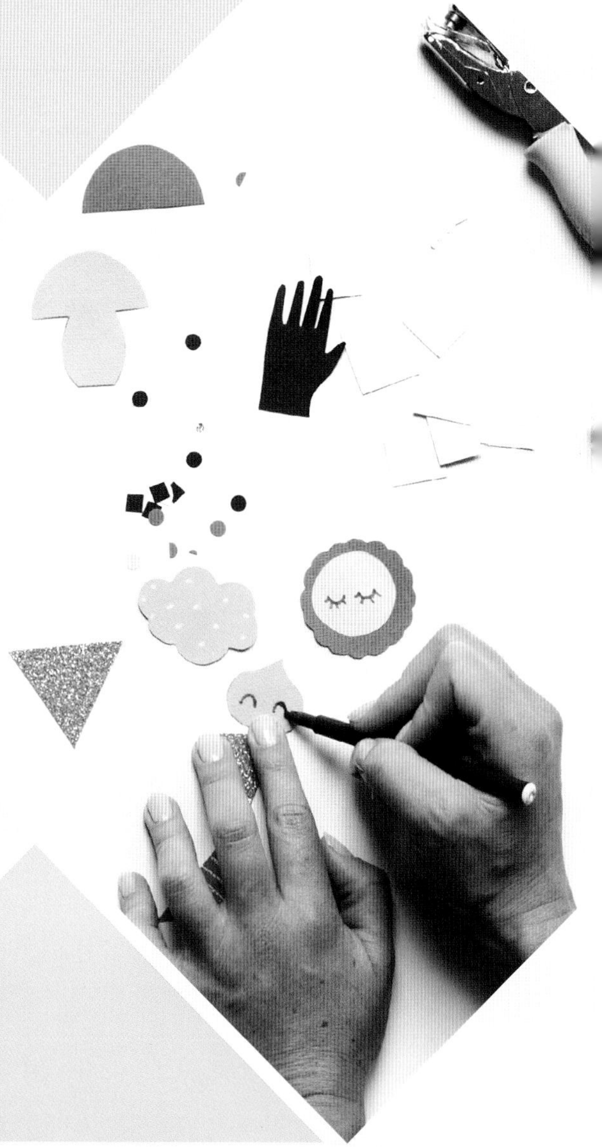

4

Stick all pieces together using double-sided adhesive tape and paper glue. Cut a small square of the mount board for each item and place it on the back where the magnet will go (this will give the assembly a bit of extra strength). Stick magnets to the back of each one.

5

Put your magnet friends to work!

PAINT YOUR OWN PLATES

Who needs an expensive dinner set when you can buy
some not-so-expensive-plates (op shop ones, even) and some
porcelain paint pens and make your own? Seriously, I loved putting
this project together. So much so I ended up with more plates than I could
put in the book. Tyke and Ari got in on the action too: Ari drew a cat with a machine
gun on his plate and Tyke drew his favourite computer game character. Awesome.
I went a bit more designer-y for mine (surprise, surprise). I chose three colours and mixed
and matched colours and motifs. But even the plates used to test out the pens looked great. Then
all you have to do is let them dry, bake them and they will last a long time. They may even become family
heirlooms. This could work as an activity for a kids' party too, or an adults' party for that matter. Everybody
who came across these in my studio wanted to have a go!

YOU WILL NEED

◦ 4 plain white plates

◦ porcelain paint pens (I used gold, pink and blue)

◦ pencil

◦ oven

Difficulty:
Easy

1

Wipe down the plates and make sure they are clean: the pens will work best on the cleanest plates possible.

HERE WE GO

3

Pencil the designs onto the plates.

2

If you have a spare plate, have a bit of a play around to test your motifs and get used the pens.

It's a good idea to sketch out some of your design ideas in a sketchbook before using paint pens on plates. It can also make for a nice picture!

ZOOM...

TRIANGLES

SILVER?

SQUARES

GOLD

Go over the pencil designs with the porcelain pens. I found the pens worked best with lines rather than filling in larger solid shapes, but both look good. I also found the different coloured inks had different coverage (for example, pink was really good, but blue was not as good).

5

Follow the manufacturer's instructions to make the paint permanent; for example, by baking in an oven.

WOODEN BEAD TRIVET

I only recently discovered what a trivet is. I mean, I had
been using them for years, but I didn't know they actually had
a name. Now I like to use the term 'trivet' often. It's quite hard to
drop into a conversation, but I still manage. Makes me feel quite grown up
and all homewares-y. Oh, and the brilliant bead-painting technique in this project
was developed by Amelia. Great thinking, lady!

° 40 raw wooden beads: mine are 30 mm (1¼ in) diameter

° barbecue skewers

° acrylic paint and paintbrush

° satin varnish

° florists' wire (you could also use string)

Difficulty:
Medium

1

To paint the beads, first thread them onto a skewer and rest the skewer between two objects. Paint the beads in solid colours or simple patterns then leave to dry. Varnish the painted beads and allow to dry.

3

Secure these 6 beads by passing wire through the holes and twist the ends together.

2

Place a single bead in the centre and then form a circle of 6 beads around it.

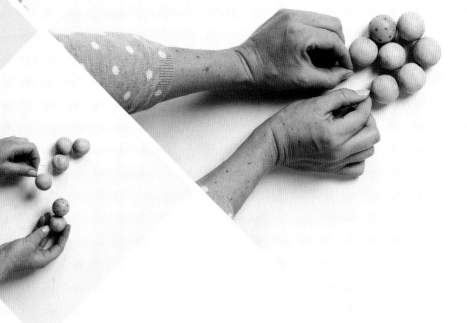

4

Secure the centre bead by passing the wire through it and tying it to the wire in the outer circle.

5

The next circle is made with 12 beads. Pass the wire through again and twist to secure. Add some wire on the underside to attach it to the inner circle.

6

The final circle is made with 18 beads. Pass the wire through and twist to secure. Add some wire on the underside to attach it to the previous two circles.

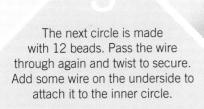

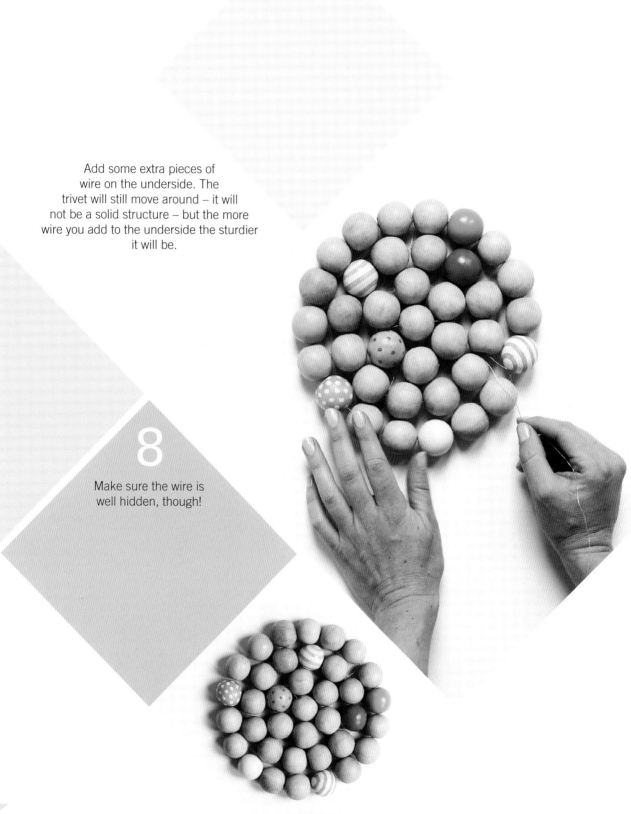

Add some extra pieces of wire on the underside. The trivet will still move around – it will not be a solid structure – but the more wire you add to the underside the sturdier it will be.

8

Make sure the wire is well hidden, though!

FRIENDLY HERB GARDEN

Lord knows I do love putting a face on things. I've added
them to some pretty strange objects too: a beer keg, shoes
and an apple, to name just a few. So, when it comes to my herbs
and pot plants, I'd like them to have faces, too. Several of them. In fact,
let's just make a whole family.

My herb garden family members include: snoozy baby brother, grumpy tween sister,
awkward geeky older brother, super happy mum (that's me) and all-round good-guy dad. Oh,
and how could I forget the most important family member: the beloved pet cat? My plan for this
family is to have them all sitting on a tray in the middle of our kitchen table so we can snap off the herbs
for use when we need, and also take them outside for easy watering when needed. That is, when we have a
kitchen that actually has some light, not the dark, cave-like one I have now. One day…

YOU WILL NEED

◦ ceramic vessels of varying sizes: I used 6 that were a mixture of new pots and op-shop finds

◦ pencil, ceramic pens (black, pink, red and blue), white paint pen

◦ selection of herbs (the pots will need at least 24 hours for the ink to
become permanent, so you may want to buy the herbs after the
pots are complete)

◦ potting mix

Difficulty:
Medium

HERE WE GO

1

Plan out your pots. Take into consideration the pot sizes and work your family characters around that. Think about different hairstyles, facial expressions and accessories.

2

Sketch the faces with a pencil before starting.

3

Make your final drawings with the ceramic pens. With most ceramic pens, if you make a mistake and the ink is still wet, you can simply wipe it away with a damp cloth.

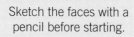

4

Follow the manufacturer's instructions so that the ink becomes permanent. Different brands use different techniques for this: one brand I used just had to air dry for 72 hours; another had to dry for 24 hours and then bake in a low-temperature oven.

6

Start snipping!

5

Pot the herbs using the potting mix.

CORK COASTERS

Until recently I've never been much of coaster user. I have plenty of them, but I always forget to take them out of the drawer and use them. This all changed after I lovingly restored our kitchen table (it was in a sad state after years of dried breakfast cereal abuse). Since then I have become quite particular about protecting the table's now beautiful surface. Enter a new coaster obsession. Working with cork is a fun thing too. It is pretty easy to come across: I bought these sheets from my local art store. It was a bit thicker than I wanted but worked out fine. I found lots of sources online too.

YOU WILL NEED

◦ Coaster template (page 211)

◦ two A4 sheets of 10 mm (⅜ in) thick cork

◦ pencil and ruler

◦ craft knife and cutting mat (if you have one)

◦ fine grit sandpaper

◦ masking tape

◦ acrylic paints and brushes or applicators

◦ acrylic clear varnish (optional)

Difficulty:
Easy

1

Copy the template shape on to the cork. Trace the outlines first.

HERE WE GO

3

Cut the shapes out using a sharp craft knife and metal ruler as a guide. If the cork is thick it can be quite an effort to cut through it!

2

Cut the template down to trace the inside lines.

4

Sandpaper off any rough edges (if your knife is super sharp, there won't be any!)

6

Paint the coasters. The cork soaks up the paint quite well, so you'll need 3–4 coats of each colour. Make sure each colour is dry before proceeding with the next.

5

Mask off the sections you want to paint. It is a good idea to do this one colour at a time; that is, all the blue parts, then all the pink parts, and so on.

ADD A LAYER OF
VARNISH IF YOUR
COASTERS ARE GOING
TO COP HEAVY USAGE.

SCRAP
PILE NAPKINS

I have been known to buy fabric just for the
colour. In fact, most of my fabric is bought this way, on
impulse. Some of it does go into making things for markets,
but I'm also perfectly happy just to have piles of (often not) neatly
stacked fabric in my shelves. It could be considered one of my favourite
things to look at. But of course, it does also take up much-needed space. So,
on the odd occasion, I have a throwing-out clean up, but there are some fabric scraps
I can't bear to part with. Here is a good way to put those special scraps to use. My napkins
are not a matching set, but I think they work together because I limited the colours to three. I have
also added patterns to the plain fabrics in these colours, using three different techniques: stamping,
bleaching and fabric markers. Adding the pattern might be going the extra mile, but it makes the project a
hundred times more fun, and the resulting set is a hundred times more special.

YOU WILL NEED

◦ fabric scraps: my napkins are 30 cm (12 in) squares, you can make yours any size depending
on the size of the fabric scraps. When cutting, remember to allow for hems ◦ fabric scissors
◦ sewing machine and sewing thread to match the fabrics ◦ iron and ironing board

For stamping:
◦ blank stamp and stamp cutting tools ◦ fabric stamping ink

For bleaching:
◦ bleach and paintbrush to apply ◦ newspaper
◦ rubber gloves

For marking:
◦ fabric markers

Difficulty:
Hard

HERE WE GO

1

For stamping fabric:
pencil your design onto
the stamp and cut it out with the
stamp cutting tools.

3

For bleaching fabric:
put on your gloves and lay
out some scrap paper. Test a
small swatch of fabric to make sure the
bleach will work on it.

Lay out the fabric (make
sure it's ironed) and stamp
the pattern on.

Wash out the paintbrush
you use for the bleach
thoroughly immediately after use;
the bleach will make the bristles brittle.

4

Lay out the fabric and
paint patterns on with
bleach. Wait 10 minutes for the
bleach to work.

For fabric markers:
test the markers on small
swatches of fabric. Use light
colours on lighter fabrics and darker
colours on medium fabrics.

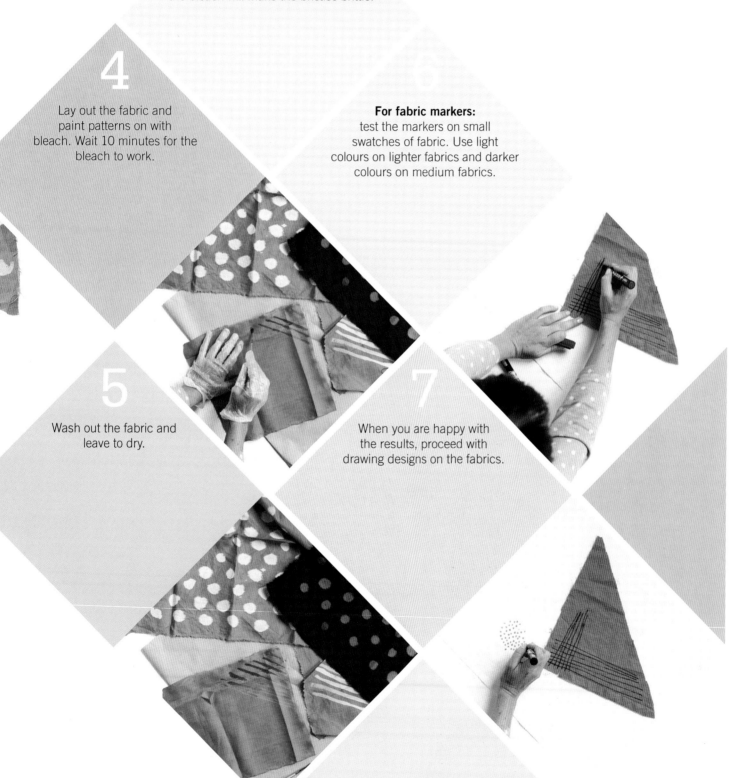

5

Wash out the fabric and
leave to dry.

7

When you are happy with
the results, proceed with
drawing designs on the fabrics.

The dotted napkin
took me quite a long time.
Sometimes the best things do,
and it's worth it in the end.

Sewing:
cut all the fabrics down
to the same size, allowing 2 cm
(¾ in) for hem allowance. Fold a double
hem and press with an iron.

9

Use a sewing machine
and matching sewing thread
to stitch the hems.

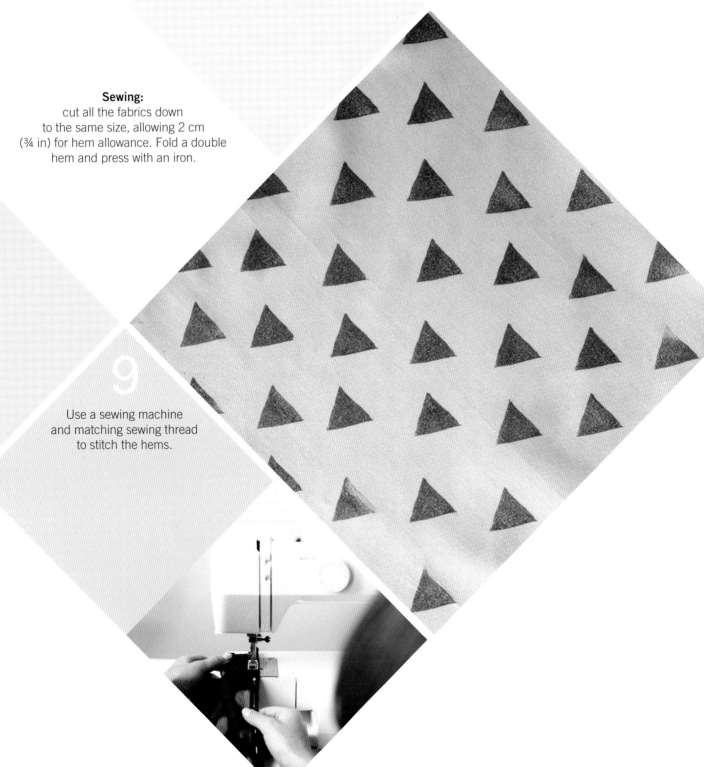

BONBONS

My family doesn't go in for Christmas in
the big traditional manner, but we still have a
nice family celebration. It's usually a casual affair,
with lots of people down at my mum's beach house, and
Raph and me cooking for everyone. It's super fun.

Despite our lack of traditions, we do love a bonbon. Who can resist a paper
hat and a cheesy joke? Not me. Here are some bonbons you can make yourself.
Not necessarily for Christmas: they can be used for any celebration. I designed them so
you would get a double dose of surprise: confetti from the outside and whatever you decide
to put on the inside, such as more confetti, pompoms, trinkets and any kind of message you prefer.
Or, of course, a cheesy joke. For extra authenticity you can also buy the 'bangers' and add them in.

YOU WILL NEED

◦ 6 cardboard toilet roll centres or any other cardboard rolls

◦ acrylic paint and paintbrush

◦ 6 mm (¼ in) circle punch

◦ coloured card and paper

◦ crepe paper

◦ clear cellophane (on the roll, if you can get it)

◦ pencil or felt-tip marker

◦ scissors and string

◦ washi tape

Difficulty:
Medium

you are cute!

HERE WE GO

1

Paint the cardboard rolls. I chose different colours for the outside and inside.

2

Make confetti for the outside using the circle punch or use the scissors to make different shapes.

3

Cut some small pieces of paper and write messages or jokes.

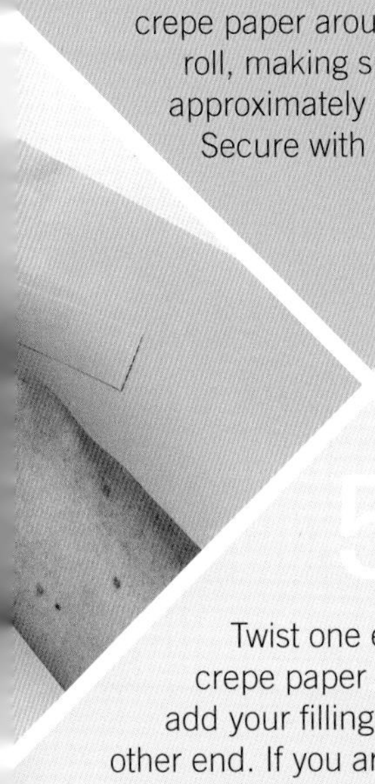

4

Cut lengths of crepe paper and cellophane. Make the cellophane slightly shorter than the crepe paper, so that when the bonbon is pulled, it is just the crepe paper (the cellophane won't tear). Wrap crepe paper around the carboard roll, making sure the roll is approximately in the middle. Secure with washi tape.

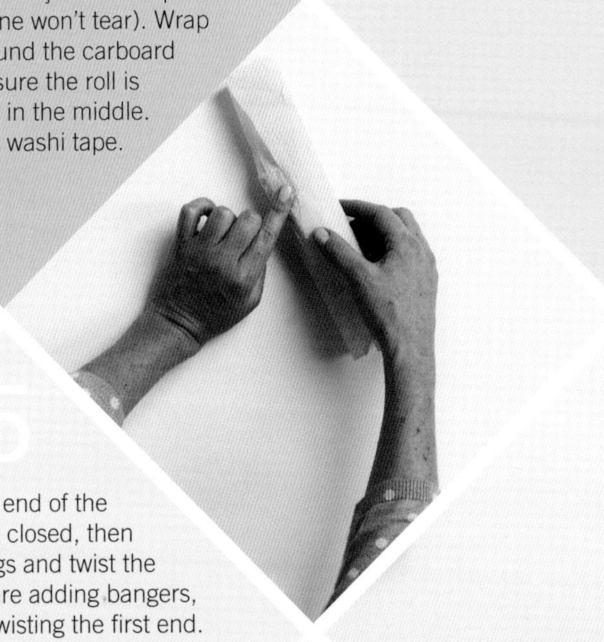

5

Twist one end of the crepe paper closed, then add your fillings and twist the other end. If you are adding bangers, insert one before twisting the first end.

6

Lay a piece of cellophane out and sprinkle on some confetti.

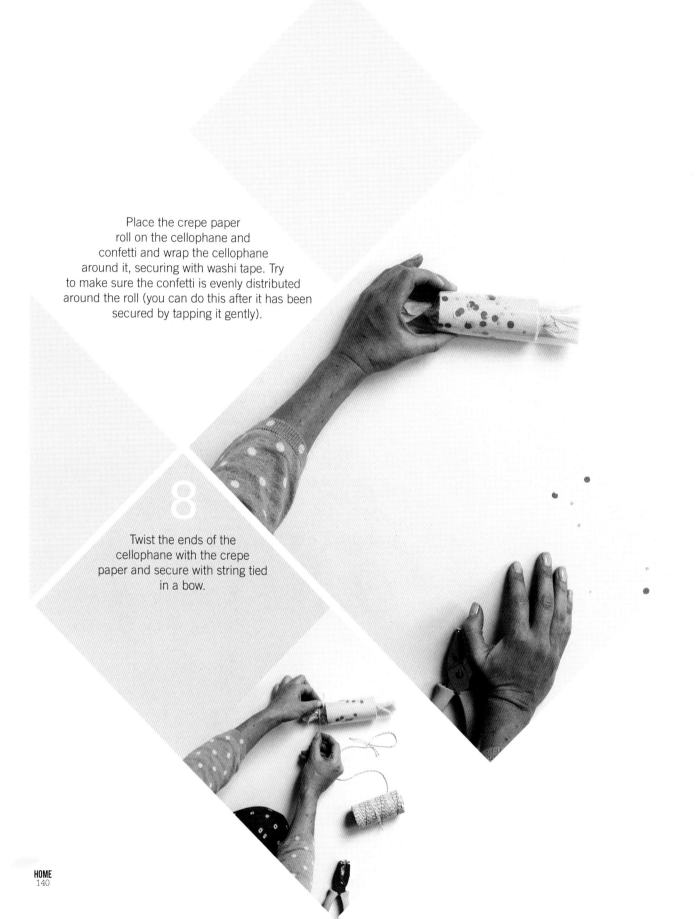

Place the crepe paper roll on the cellophane and confetti and wrap the cellophane around it, securing with washi tape. Try to make sure the confetti is evenly distributed around the roll (you can do this after it has been secured by tapping it gently).

8.

Twist the ends of the cellophane with the crepe paper and secure with string tied in a bow.

SLEEPING SPACES

MY BEDROOM IS ALWAYS A SPACE I HAVE TREASURED. LIVING IN SHARE HOUSES WHEN I WAS YOUNGER (ONE SPACE WITH FIVE OTHER PEOPLE!) MY BEDROOM WAS THE PLACE I COULD PERSONALISE THE MOST.

My bedroom walls soon filled up with postcards, textiles and even vintage clothing and shoes. In fact, my bedroom was where my first inspiration walls came to life.

Now I am all grown up (well, supposedly), and I have my own whole house to do with as I please. Our bedroom is the fanciest and nicest room in the house, complete with big windows overlooking the park, ceiling rosettes and a vintage (and very dusty) chandelier. When we first moved into our house, I would say to Raph that it was like waking up in a fancy hotel room every day.

I have surprised myself by wanting to make our bedroom quite understated compared to the rest of the house. Minimal decoration (minimal for me that is), more neutral colours and lots of blank wall space. While everywhere else has gathered more and more bits and pieces (let's not call it 'clutter' just yet), our bedroom has pretty much maintained the same level of semi-scarcity.

I'm pretty sure this has been a subconscious decision on my part to keep this room a 'retreat' from the rest of the madness of our lives. It actually works pretty well, and sometimes I can even meditate in there.

The kids' bedroom is a different story: it's colourful, with bits and pieces everywhere. They get some 'guided' free rein to choose the artworks for the walls and everything else. They are just getting big enough to want to hang out in there on their own, so I think it's all about to undergo another change in the near future. I wonder how many older boys' bedroom DIY projects I can force them into?

A bit about mess: our house is, more often than not, in a chaotic state. This is not by choice; once upon a time I lived in a house that was clean. I cleaned it regularly. I liked the cleanliness, too. These days, I feel like that clean person is trapped inside a messy family. I also often blame my hoarding gene, and our very busy lives. (If there is a choice between playing a game of Uno with my kids and putting away dishes, guess which one I'm going to pick?)

My other often-called-upon excuse is that the messiness represents creativity. It sounds appropriate, but actually I don't think it's true.

I do relish our house being clean, and endeavour to clean it when I can. Unfortunately, within ten minutes of it being cleaned, it is hit by the whirlwind that is my kids and we are back to where we started.

So instead of mess being a point of constant frustration, I have resolved to accept the fact that a bit of mess is actually another thing that now makes my house a home.

SLEEPING
SPACES
PROJECTS

Here are some
things you can
make to create an extra special
space in your bedroom. I encourage
you to personalise them even more
– change the colours of the piñata to
match your favourite doona cover, or
change the shape of the mobile so it
fits your bedroom window just right
– and make them as much
'you' as you can!

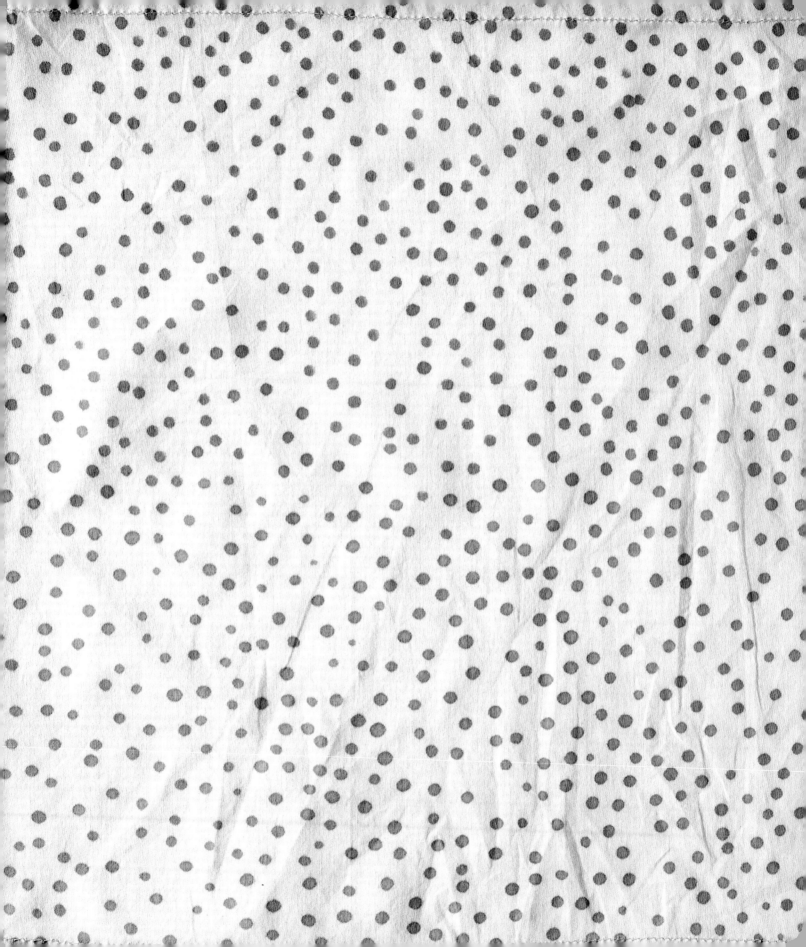

BRAIDED
RAG RUG

My crafty gran used to make these rugs and had them
scattered around her house. She used scrap fabrics for hers.
I had good intentions of also using scraps, but then the designer in
me came out and I simply had to have specific colours that my scraps did
not contain. I started with one fabric I already had, and then bought a few new
ones to go with it. A craft warning: this project takes a while. Not just have-a-few-cups-
of-tea while: I'm talking days here. Weeks even! You might also need a bit of space. But it's
meditative and if you take your time you will have something large and beautiful that could last
for generations.

YOU WILL NEED

◦ fabric cut into strips around 10 cm (4 in) wide x a workable length (1.5–2 m or about 2 yards), although
I was quite loose with my cutting. The amount of fabric will vary depending on how big you want the
rug, and also the type of fabric you use. I used around 10 m (11 yards) of fabric.

◦ sewing machine (optional)

◦ needle and thread

◦ bulldog clip

◦ pins

Difficulty:
Hard

HERE WE GO

Take three strips of fabric and sew them together with a row of stitching at one end.

3

Braid the three strips together.

2

Place the sewn ends of fabric in a bulldog clip and hang the clip on a nail or hook (preferably head-height or higher). You can also braid by holding the fabric between your knees.

4

When you are starting to run out of fabric to braid, sew a new fabric strip to the end of each of the first ones with a row of stitching.
Adjust the position of the bulldog clip to near the start of the new strips and continue braiding.

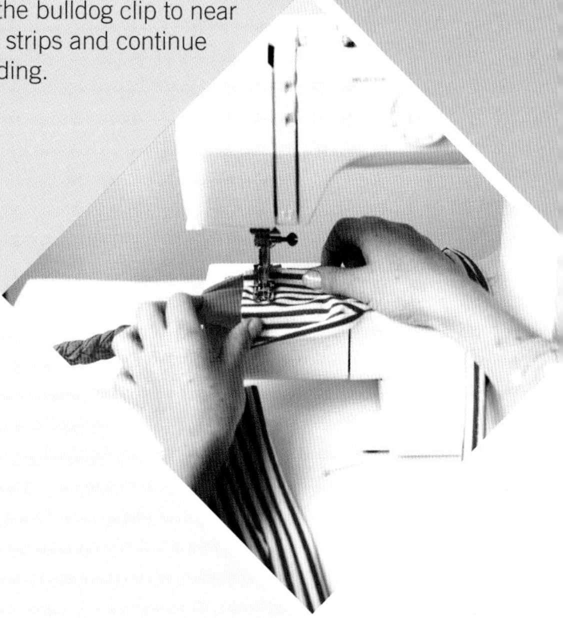

I used stretch fabric for
this rug. After a few tests I
found it much easier to work with,
and it also made the resulting rug softer
and bouncier.

Continue until all of the
fabric strips are used up (for
my rug, I had about 10 m or
11 yards of braided fabric).

6

Construct the rug:
I found the best way was
pinning small sections together as
you go, and then stitching the
underside of the braids together. You
will need quite a few stitches to keep it
together. To finish, stitch down the end
of the braid into the previous round.

COSMIC
MOTH LAMP

This project was born out of desperation, as
some of the best things often are. Ari doesn't like the
dark, and it was an aesthetic challenge to find him some
kind of night-light or lamp that we both liked and wasn't hideously
ugly. So I set about making one that we would both like. That being
said, the parts for this project can be tricky to find: a lampshade frame is no
problem, but the lamp component with an on/off switch is hard. Best option I found
was buying a cheap lamp and disassembling it. Another word of warning: make sure you
buy paper that is suitable for lamps. Using the wrong paper can mean fire ... And that is very bad.
I bought mine from an art store, which had a great range of lamp-suitable papers.

YOU WILL NEED

◦ cylinder-shape lampshade frame

◦ light bulb fitting with on/off switch (see above)

◦ 1 sheet of fire-retardant paper suitable for lampshades

◦ spray paint (dark blue and very dark navy)

◦ Cosmic Moth Lamp templates (page 208)

◦ coloured card

◦ scissors, ruler and pencil

◦ PVA glue and paintbrush

◦ pins and pegs

Difficulty:
Medium

HERE WE GO

1

Measure your lampshade frame and work out how much paper you will need. The paper will wrap around the frame, plus 2 cm (¾ in) overlap and approximately 3 cm (1¼ in) extra at the top and bottom to fold over the frame.

2

Cut the paper to these measurements. Rule the fold lines along the top and bottom edges of the paper.

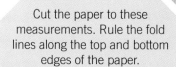

3

Spray the paper with dark blue spray paint. The paper I used was quite thick, but I still wanted some of the white to show through (it added to my cosmic look), so I only did one coat, and only on one side of the paper. Thick paper can take a while to dry.

4

Once the first coat of paint is dry, add some spots of dark navy blue.

5

Cut out paper shapes
and moth pieces.

7

Pencil some clouds on
the back (unpainted) side of
the lamp paper. Use a pin to prick
around the shapes and create a line of
pinpricks that you will see when the light is
turned on.

6

Decorate moth pieces
and stick them together
using PVA glue.

8

Stick on all the cut-out
shapes except the moth,
using PVA glue.

9

Along the borders of the paper (the part that will fold under), make cuts at 5 cm (2 in) intervals, cutting down to the ruled fold line.

11

Starting on the top edge of the lamp, fold over each section of the border and glue it down, placing a peg on each section to keep it in place as you go.

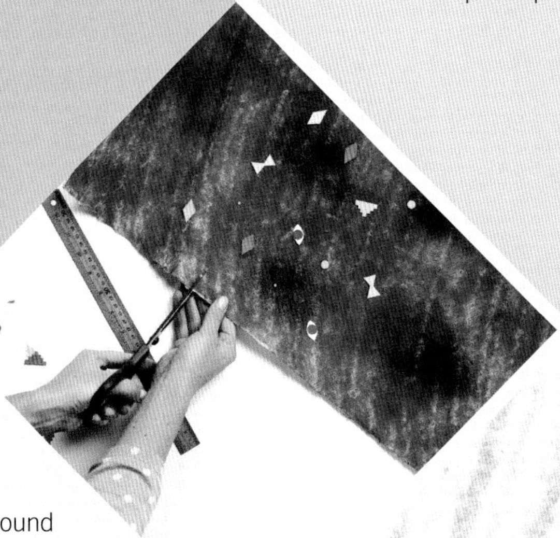

Wrap the paper around the lampshade frame and use one of the pegs to hold it in place at the beginning.

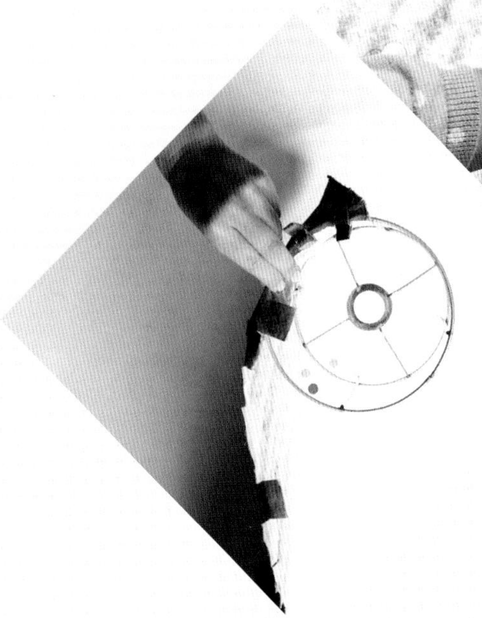

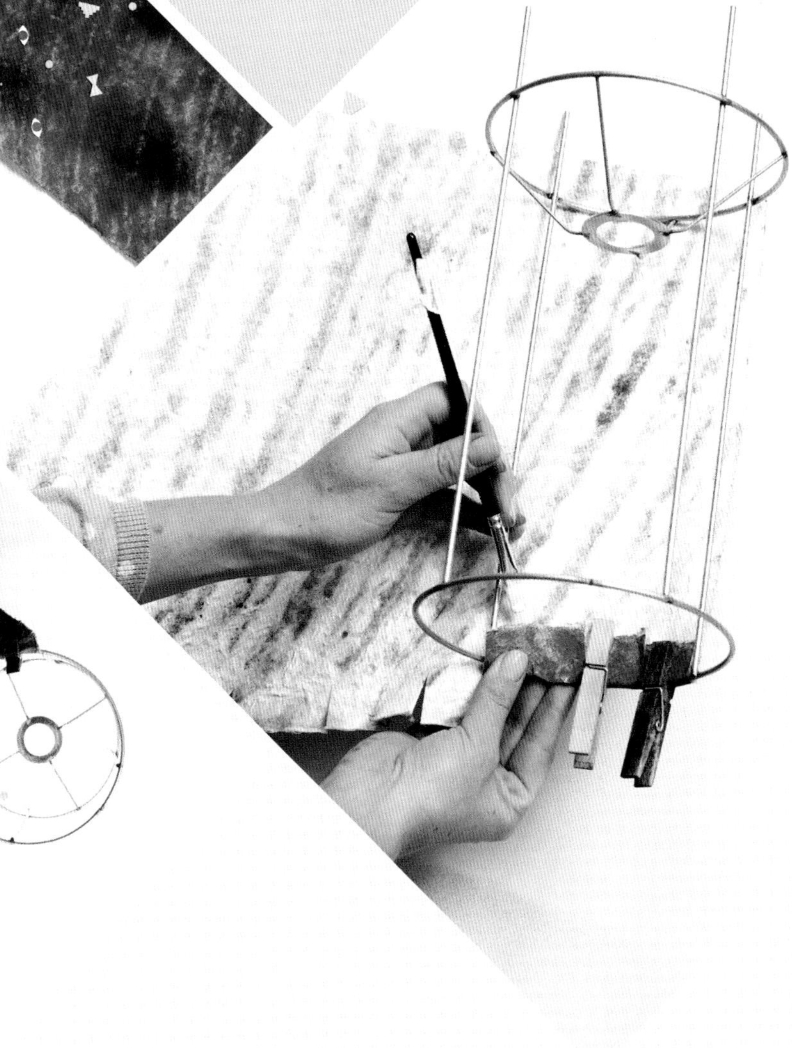

Once the top edge is finished, do the same with the bottom of the shade. Finally, glue the side join. You might have to hold this in place with pegs and also your fingers for a few minutes while the glue is bonding.

13

Add the moth near the top of the lampshade. Add the light globe fitting.

MOBILE

If you have seen my first book,
Find & Keep, you will know that it also
contained a mobile project. Well, my love for
mobiles has not subsided, so here is another one.
This one is a bit more free-form, using bits of nature. If you
follow my instructions you will get something close to the one
I have made, but I would encourage you to make your own version.
Once you have selected your sticks, play around with shapes and other bits
and pieces and see what will work best. I used driftwood for my mobile as it is light
and floats nicely in the breeze too, but any sticks you find can work well.

YOU WILL NEED

◦ 2 sticks: I chose one around 35 cm (14 in) and one around 20 cm (8 in)

◦ double-sided adhesive tape and PVA glue

◦ embroidery thread

◦ Mobile templates (page 207)

◦ coloured paper or card (small pieces are fine) and scissors

◦ small wooden beads

◦ acrylic paint and paintbrush

◦ washi tape in different patterns

◦ small circle punch (optional)

◦ 2 pompoms

Difficulty:
Easy

HERE WE GO

1
Add some double-sided adhesive tape to the sections of the sticks where you would like to wrap the embroidery thread.

3
Cut out the paper shapes and paint the beads.

2
Wrap the sticks with embroidery thread. Take your time doing this to make sure each wrap of thread goes exactly beside the previous one. This will make it look beautiful and even.

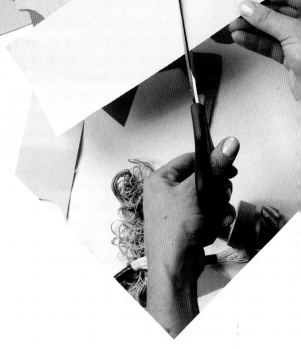

4

Decorate the paper shapes using paint, washi tape, and by gluing smaller shapes (such as punched circles) to form a pattern.

6

Lay the pieces of thread out and work out what pieces and materials will go on each: paper shapes, pompoms and beads.

5

Roughly measure and cut lengths of embroidery thread to hang the decorations, keeping in mind where you would like each piece to be.

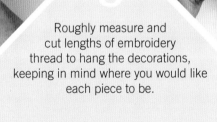

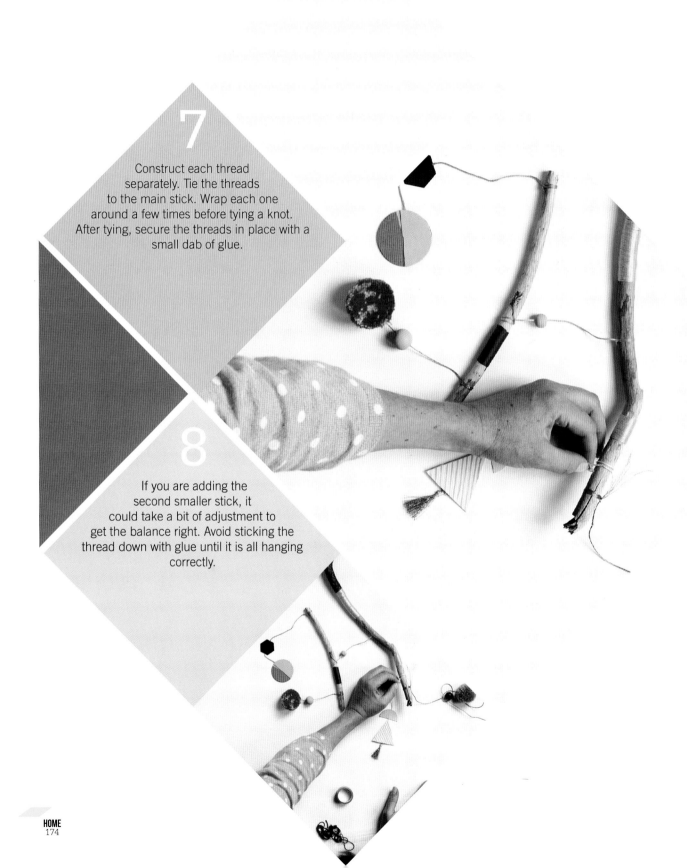

7

Construct each thread separately. Tie the threads to the main stick. Wrap each one around a few times before tying a knot. After tying, secure the threads in place with a small dab of glue.

8

If you are adding the second smaller stick, it could take a bit of adjustment to get the balance right. Avoid sticking the thread down with glue until it is all hanging correctly.

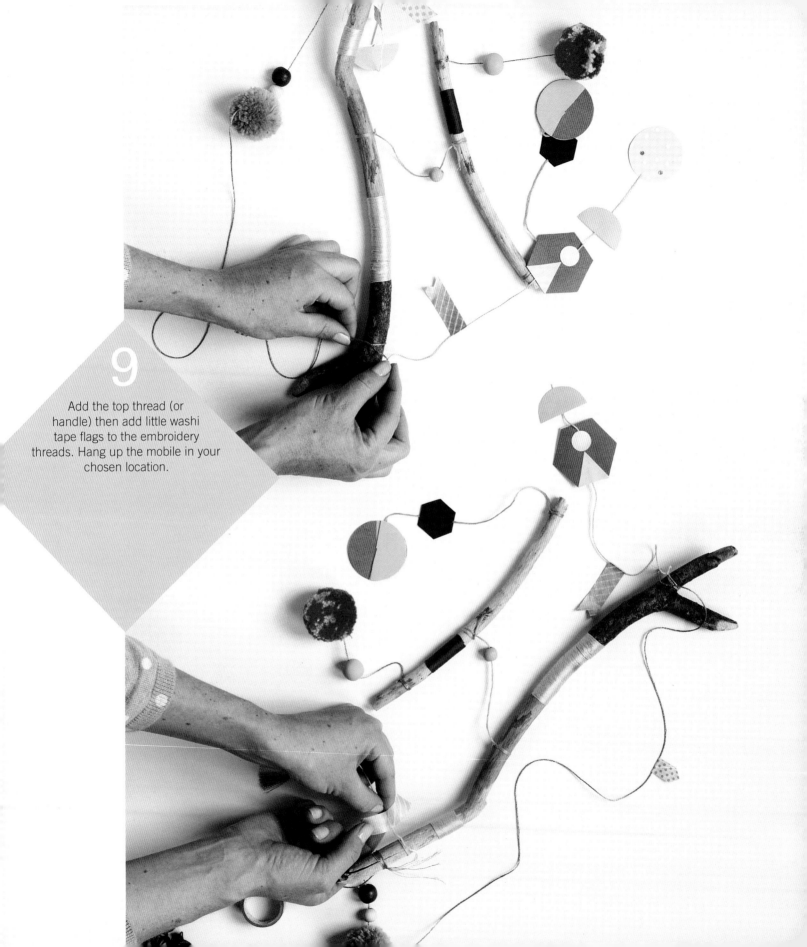

9

Add the top thread (or handle) then add little washi tape flags to the embroidery threads. Hang up the mobile in your chosen location.

EMBROIDERED CUSHION

There is cushion overload at our house. In fact, one could
say you can't find my bed for the cushions. But I like it that way.
Tyke and Ari like it too: is there much more fun for a child than to dive
head-first into a pile of cushions? I think not. And that way I can kid myself
the cushions serve an actual purpose too. I have written before about my love of
embroidery. This one is a slightly bigger project than the embroidery project in *Find & Keep*,
and will take decidedly longer. This project also involves (shock! horror!) some basic sewing at the
end. But don't worry, it's very basic. Even I managed to do it.

YOU WILL NEED

Cushion:
◦ 2 fabric panels approximately 40 cm (16 in) square ◦ pins ◦ sewing machine and sewing thread ◦
cushion stuffing or cushion insert ◦ needle and thread

Embroidery:
◦ Embroidered Cushion templates (page 206) ◦ iPad with lightbox app or
a window ◦ embroidery thread in several colours ◦ embroidery hoop
(15 cm/6 in is a good size for this project) ◦ crewel embroidery
needle ◦ pencil

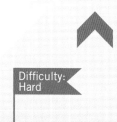

Difficulty:
Hard

HERE WE GO

Trace the design from the template onto one of the pieces of fabric. You can do this with a lightbox or by taping the template and fabric to a sunlit window.

3

For the stars I used star stitch.

2

It's completely up to you where you start this embroidery, but I suggest you start with the simpler parts, and work up to the more detailed ones. I used a simple running stitch for the cross and small circle, and backstitch for the outline of the hand. (A stitch guide can be found on page 207).

4

For the diamond, semicircle and the triangle nose, I used a satin stitch to fill up the shapes from one end to the other.

5

For the dodecahedron, the eyes and the stepped shape I used a long and short satin stitch.

6

I used smaller double stitches (also known as seed stitch) as dots in the stepped shape.

With the embroidery complete, it's time to sew your cushion. Pin the edges together and sew a 2 cm (¾ in) seam around all four sides, leaving a 15 cm (6 in) gap in the bottom side of the cushion, so you can add your stuffing.

8

Once the cushion has been stuffed to your liking, hand sew the cushion closed with tiny stitches.

POMPOM
BLANKET

Although I do love a blanket, I like the way they look
folded and stacked even better (especially if there are a few
quilts in there too – perfect!) The blankets do get put to good use
too. Twelve-foot ceilings and a distinct lack of heating in our home means
it's freezing come winter, and many layers are required if one wants to laze about
on the couch. I also love the idea of taking something from a thrift store and adding a
few things to make it all your own. I was influenced by Moroccan pompom blankets for this
project. I was desperate for one, but my budget didn't agree, so I made my own, more colourful,
version. There are so many options you could try to customise your own blanket: adding trims, cutting and
adding new panels or embroidered patches (like those great Girl-Guide blankets) just to name a few.

YOU WILL NEED

◦ blanket

◦ woollen yarn

◦ plastic yarn needle

◦ pompoms

◦ pins

Difficulty:
Easy

1

Spread out your blanket and work out what you would like to do. I kept mine simple with stitching and pompom trims, but I matched the colours to the existing blanket to tie it all together.

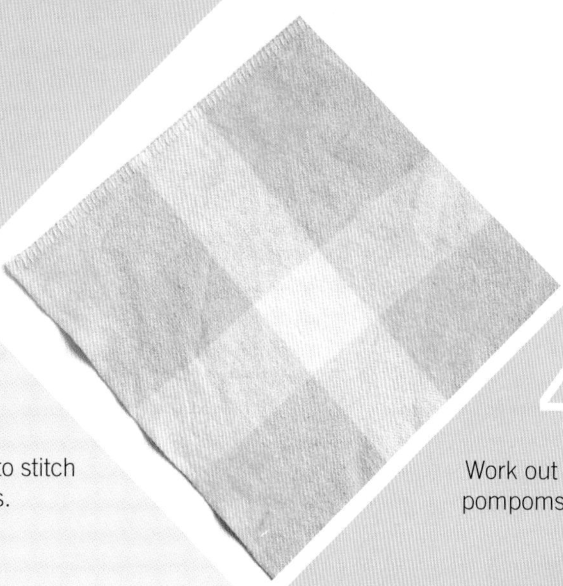

HERE WE GO

Stitch simple crosses in woollen yarn using a tacking stitch.

2

Mark out areas to stitch using pins.

4

Work out how many pompoms you need.

5

Make pompoms, or buy
them ready-made.

Stitch on pompoms
using woollen yarn. I used a
cluster of larger ones on
the corners.

JUMPING
JACKETTE

As part of my job, I often get to design characters.
Jackette did the classic run-away-from-home-at-16 to
join the circus. Circus life embraced her and she inevitably
became an acrobatic star, but always wears a mask to hide her
identity from the authorities. She also sews all her own clothes, has a
pet ferret and her favourite colour is silver. Jackette has a few fiddly bits to put
together, but once assembled this teenage runaway will twist and turn and jump at
your command. I have her hanging in my bedroom window and I like her a lot. Please be
gentle with her though: she is not designed for rough handling.

YOU WILL NEED

◦ card: navy, blue, hot pink, lilac, aqua, pale pink, yellow and silver, and a small piece of thick card for the body

◦ Jumping Jackette templates (page 201)

◦ scissors or craft knife and small circle punch (optional)

◦ paper glue, paintbrush and pencil

◦ 6 split-pin brads

◦ small tassel

◦ 2 small wooden beads

◦ string and tape

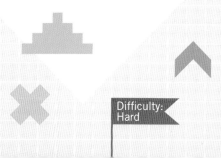

Difficulty:
Hard

1

Cut all the pieces out as indicated on the templates. Don't forget to add the string holes on the arm and leg pieces (I used a circle punch for these).

Add the yellow strips to the legs and body to form a pattern and glue on the feet. I've chosen to do this with tiny pieces of paper because I like that kind of torture, but you could also use a pencil or paint.

2

Glue the card body to the paper body.

4

Add hands to the lower ends of the arms, and then join the bottom half of the arm to the top half with the split-pin brads.

5

Make the face:
stick the neck piece to the
face piece, then insert the face
piece into the slit on the hair piece and
secure at the back only.

6

Add the mask and hat.
Add spots to the hat. Draw
on a mouth with pencil.
Then, attach the face to the body at
the neck. Make sure you stick the neck
to the back of the body.

7

Attach the legs at the
back of the body using
split-pin brads.

Attach the arms to the
back of the body using
split-pin brads.

9

Thread a small piece of string into the holes at the top of the arms and secure. Do the same with the legs.

10

Tie a longer piece of string from the middle of the string joining the arms to the middle of the string joining the legs, and leave a tail hanging at least as long as the whole puppet.

11

Attach the beads and tassel to the end of the tail of string then attach the ruffle to the top of the body (don't put glue on the brads underneath or they won't work!)

12

Attach a length of string to the head for your jumping jackette to hang up.

PULL ON THE
STRING TO
MAKE YOUR
JACKETTE
JUMP

PIÑATA

I have placed piñatas in the Sleeping
Spaces section for a reason. These are not the
type of piñatas to be bashed about (although they
could easily be). I think I have been scarred for life after
a few kids' parties involving near-death piñata incidents: whose
idea was it to give a three-year-old a huge stick to swing around while
blindfolded, anyway? This piñata is strictly for decoration: something pretty
to hang in your bedroom. I like metallic paper to add a bit of shininess: the light
bounces off it with a disco ball effect (although much more subdued). The way the metallic
paper combines with the delicate crepe is nice too. Oh, and big ups to Confetti System in New
York: they are at the forefront of turning piñatas from everyday objects into things of beauty.

YOU WILL NEED

◦ crepe paper cut into 5 cm (2 in) strips, or streamers

◦ metallic cellophane or tissue paper

◦ scissors, craft knife, ruler and cutting mat

◦ Piñata template (page 211)

◦ heavy card or box board

◦ double-sided adhesive tape or glue

◦ rope

◦ masking tape

Difficulty:
Medium

HERE WE GO

Cut even slits into one long edge of the strips of crepe and metallic paper to create the fringe effect.

3

Fold and stick both pieces to form a pyramid shape.

2

Cut and score the card where indicated on the template. You will need two pieces: one for the top and one for the bottom.

4

On the top piece, make sure you leave a small hole for the rope. Insert the rope and knot it on the inside to keep it from pulling through.

If you do want to smash
the piñata, make it out of
lighter weight card or pasteboard.

Stick the top piece and
bottom piece together with
masking tape. (If this were a
piñata that was going to get smashed,
this is the part where you would cut a
flap in the top and insert any treats.)

6

Add the rows of cut
crepe paper strips. Start
from the bottom of the shape with
a line of double-sided adhesive tape,
adding the crepe paper on top. Trim the
strips to size as you go. I used a different
colour for each side.

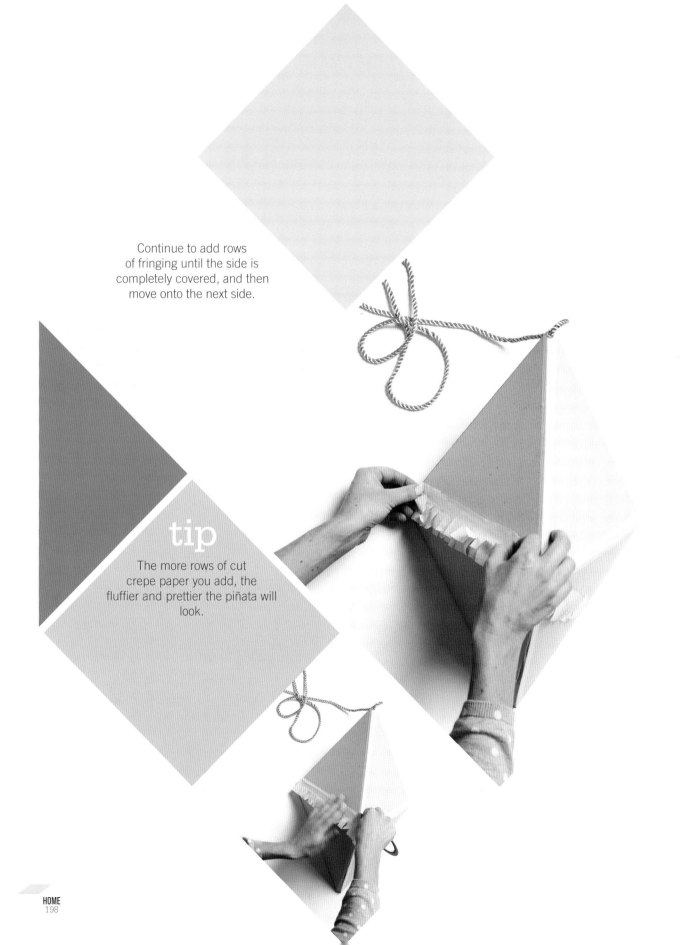

Continue to add rows
of fringing until the side is
completely covered, and then
move onto the next side.

tip

The more rows of cut
crepe paper you add, the
fluffier and prettier the piñata will
look.

OJOS DE DIOS

Like many of you, I have fond memories of making
these when I was a kid, but it wasn't until writing this
book that I discovered these 'God's eyes' also have much
history and meaning. Here I was assuming it was something made
by the ladies at church, but I found out that they were originally made by
the indigenous peoples of America. They symbolised things such as the power
of seeing and understanding that which is unknown and unknowable. Put that in your
craft pipe and smoke it. I also read that *Ojos de Dios* were a family tradition: a central 'eye'
was made by the father when a child was born, and then a new eye was added for each year of
life until the child was five. It was seen as a form of protection. It makes them extra-awesome, if you ask
me. Regardless, they are fun and easy to make, and look super nice en masse on a wall.

◦ 2 sticks (I used sticks I found in the craft shop but they also look nice using twigs)

◦ woollen yarn in different colours

◦ scissors

◦ pompoms (optional)

Difficulty:
Easy

1

Place the sticks together at right angles to form an 'x'.

3

Wrap the woollen yarn over and around one of the sticks, then continue to the next one. Pull the wool tight between each stick. Make sure you wrap all the yarn in the same direction, and keep pushing the yarn towards the centre so you get a fuller looking 'eye'.

2

Tie one end of the woollen yarn around the meeting point of the sticks to hold them together. You might want to bind it a few times to make sure it's secure.

Tassels and beads can also look nice on Ojos de Dios.

Continue until the sticks are just about full, then tie off the ends of the yarn and tuck them behind.

5

Add pompoms to the ends of the sticks. I simply tied them on, but you could also use hot glue to attach them.

TEMPLATES

SQUARE BOX SHELF
Increase or decrease size according to your design.

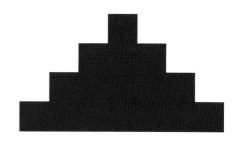

EMBROIDERED CUSHION
Increase shapes to 160% on photocopier.
Shapes appear in the same composition as shown
on cushion. Please refer to stitch guide opposite.

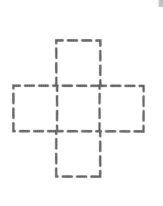
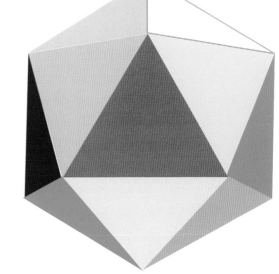

EMBROIDERY STITCH GUIDE

Back Stitch

Seed Stitch

Running Stitch

Star Stitch

Satin Stitch

Long & Short Stitch

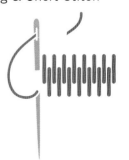

Cut 1 coloured
card

Cut 1 thicker
card

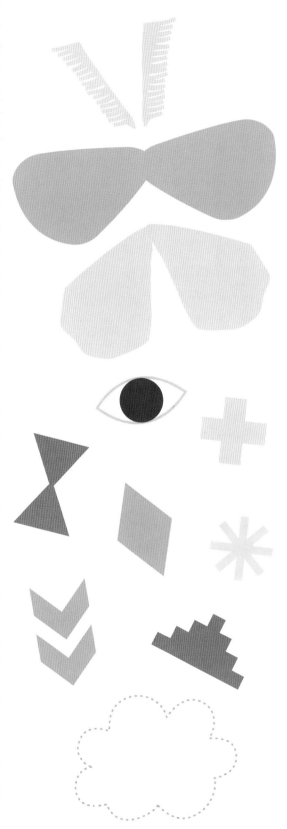

PAPER PATCHWORK

Increase shapes to 120% on photocopier.

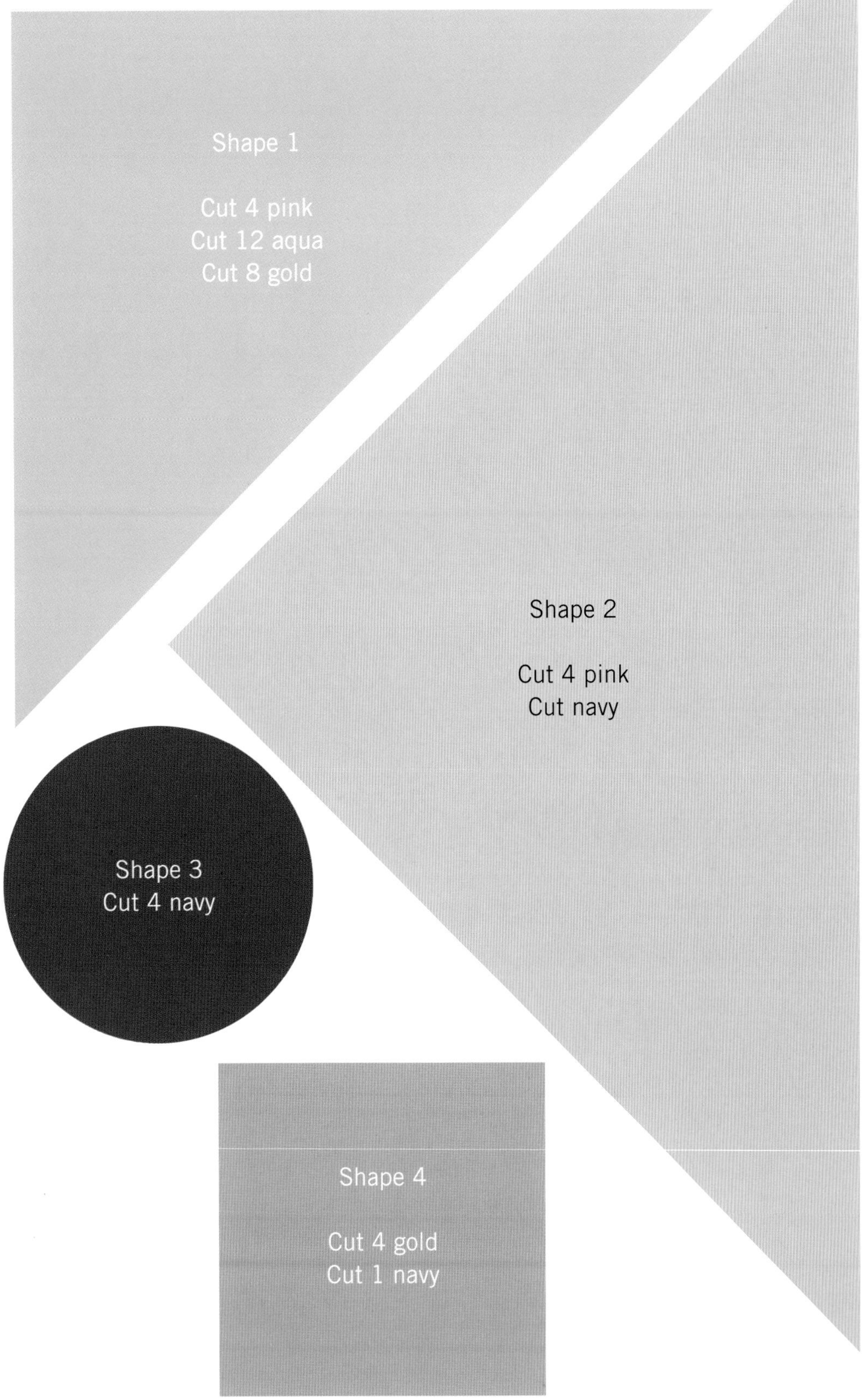
Shape 1
Cut 4 pink
Cut 12 aqua
Cut 8 gold
Shape 2
Cut 4 pink
Cut navy
Shape 3
Cut 4 navy
Shape 4
Cut 4 gold
Cut 1 navy

WALL DECOR

Shapes are 100% in size.

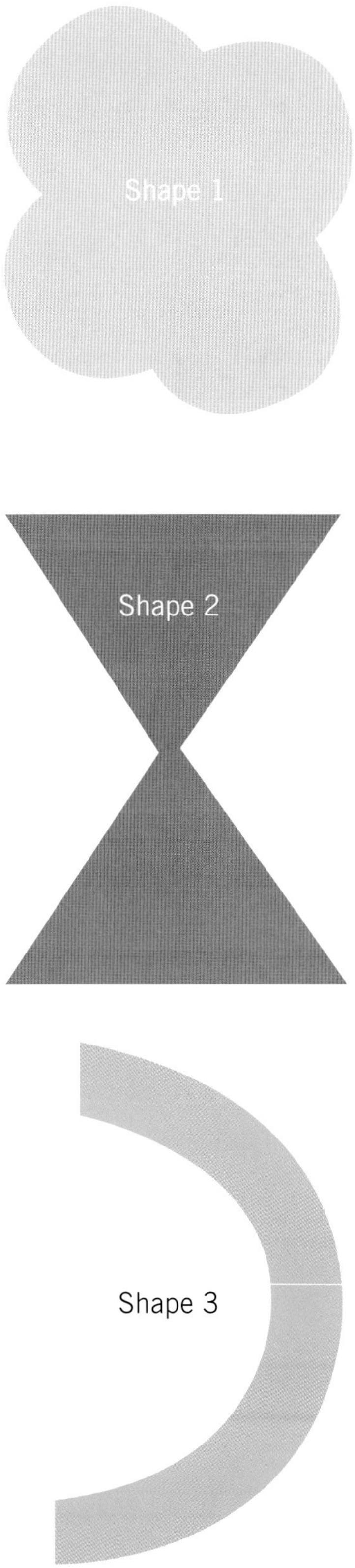
Shape 1
Shape 2
Shape 3

FOREVER CACTUS
Increase shapes to
120% on photocopier

Cactus 1

Cactus 1

Cactus 1

Cactus 1

Cactus 1

Cactus 2

Cactus 2

Cactus 3

Cactus 3

Cactus 1

Cactus 1

Cactus 3

FRIDGE MAGNETS, PINATA AND CORK COASTER

Fridge Magnets and Coaster 100% size.
Increase Piñata triangle to 130%
on photocopier.

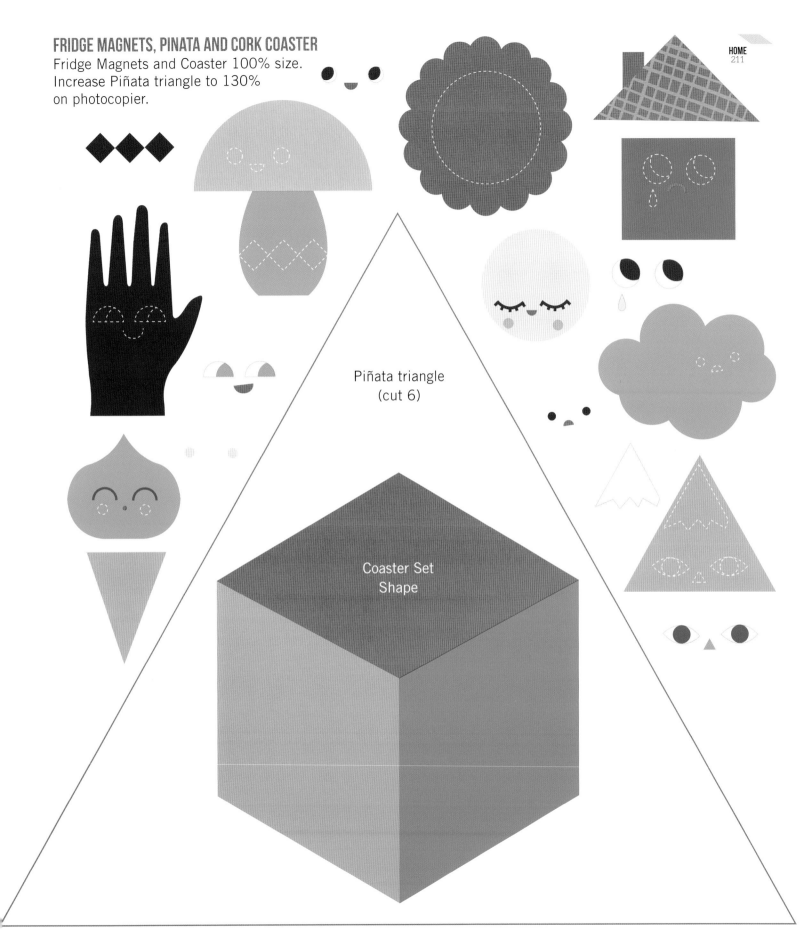

Piñata triangle
(cut 6)

Coaster Set
Shape

RESOURCES

Art and Craft Supplies

Bunnings Warehouse
bunnings.com.au

Create for Less (US)
createforless.com

Daiso
daisostore.com.au
daisojapan.com

Dick Blick Art Materials (US)
www.dickblick.com

Ebay
ebay.com

Etsy
etsy.com

Fred Aldous (UK)
fredaldous.co.uk

IKEA
ikea.com

Loft (Japan)
loft.co.jp

Pearl Paint (US)
pearlpaint.com

Riot Art & Craft
riotstores.com.au

Spotlight
spotlight.com.au

Tokyu Hands (Japan)
tokyu-hands.co.jp

Fabric And Trims

Clegs
clegs.com.au

Lincraft
lincraft.com.au

Spoonflower
spoonflower.com

Yarn and Thread

Pickles
pickles.no

The Thread Studio
thethreadstudio.com

Webs (US)
yarn.com

Yarn + Co
yarnandco.com

Fine Art and Paper

Deans Art
deansart.com.au

Eckersley's Art & Craft
eckersleys.com.au

Melbourne Artists' Supplies
+61 3 9553 3663

Neil's Art Store
e-artstore.net

Paperpoint
paperpoint.com.au

Stationery and Washi Tape

NoteMaker
notemaker.com

Present /&/ Correct
presentandcorrect.com

Upon A Fold
uponafold.com.au

Rubber Stamps

Yellow Owl Workshop
yellowowlworkshop.com

House Tour Sites

Apartment Therapy
apartmenttherapy.com

Freunde von Freunden
freundevonfreunden.com

Slanted Mansion
slantedmansion.com

The Selby
theselby.com

The Socialite Family
thesocialitefamily.com

Inspiration

Blood & Champagne
bloodandchampagne.com

Color Collective
color-collective.blogspot.com.au

Fine Little Day
finelittleday.com

Frankie
frankie.com.au/blogs

Good Things
jorpins.blogspot.com.au

Hello Sandwich
hellosandwich.blogspot.com.au

Intelligent Clashing
intelligent-----clashing.com

It's Nice That
itsnicethat.com

Lena Corwin
blog.lenacorwin.com

Meet Me at Mikes
meetmeatmikes.com

Pinterest
pinterest.com

Remodelista
remodelista.com

Share Design
sharedesign.com

Sight Unseen
sightunseen.com

Simple Things
simpleprecious.blogspot.com.au

Thank You, Ok
thankyouok.blogspot.com.au

The Brick House
the-brick-house.com

The Design Files
thedesignfiles.net

Interiors Magazines

Anthology
anthologymag.com

Apartamento
apartamentomagazine.com

Casa BRUTUS (Japan)
casabrutus.com

Come home! (Japan)
baum-kuchen.net

Elle Decoration (UK)
elledecoration.co.uk

Habitus
habitusliving.com

Inside Out
homelife.com.au/magazine/
inside+out/

Kinfolk
kinfolk.com

Milk Decoration
milkmagazine.net

World of Interiors
worldofinteriors.co.uk

Nice Things for Your House

Anthropologie
anthropologie.com

Areaware
areaware.myshopify.com

Craft Victoria
craft.org.au/buy/shop

Ganim's Store
ganimstore.com.au

General store
shop-generalstore.com

Habitat
habitat.co.uk

Harvest Textiles
harvesttextiles.com.au

Hay
hay.dk

Mr Kitly
mrkitly.com.au

Muji
muji.net

Third Drawer Down
thirddrawerdown.com

Urban Outfitters
urbanoutfitters.com

Don't forget your local op shop, flea or craft market too. Shop and support local whenever you can!

THANK YOU

Raph: thanks for living through and staying married to me for another book.

Tyke and Ari: for helping me with my ideas and giving me inspiration. The rest of my fam: Mum, Dad, Erwin, Julie, Emily, Sean, Leslie, Joe, Sam, Rudin, Brooke, Zeddy, Joh, Andie, Annie and Norm.

Greg Hatton and Katie Marx and Hazel for letting us take over Butterland for a week. It is a magical place and made all the more amazing with you guys in it. Also thanks to Matt Green, Steamer and Sleeper (RIP).

Michelle Mackintosh: thanks for getting me through book two and helping me again with holistic book design 101. Your knowledge and friendship is so amazing and special. Steve Wide and Brontë – you guys are pretty great too.

Chris Middleton: for once again taking such beautiful photos and for always going above and beyond.

Alice Oehr: from work experience student to partner in crime – you rule, lady. Thanks for all your help over the past few months. And for letting me borrow your camera too.

My lovely helpers who I call on at various occasions: Alice Oehr, Kristina Sabarodin, Natalie Turnbull, Elise Wilkins, Amelia Leuzzi.

BS club ladies.

My very kind friends who let me photograph their houses (or sent me their own photographs): Kirra and Lulu; Alice; Nat and Frank; Elise; Tristian and Adriana; Max and Rosie; Bree and Julian; Amanda, Conor and Bonnie; Natalie; Emily and Sean; Michelle and Steve; Jess from Okologi.

My other equally-as-kind friends: Shauna, Misha and Odi; Ed, Liv, Sofia and Milo; Lawrence; Diana; Sue, Marta and Claude; Masmai, Goro, Mei and Teppei; Di and BT; Nat, Matt and Lily-bell; Leah; Daniela; Sebo, Lou, Ivy and Rocco; Lisa, Dean, Pepa and Hazel; Elska, Marcus and Izzi; Miso and Ghostpatrol; Dan and Justine; Kat, Cam and Jimmy; Kristina and Aidyl; Risa; Tai; Adeline and Rohan; Sheena and Beno; Kiah; Charlotte and Chris; Rae and Sunday; Brendan and Ellen; Cat Rabbit and Callum; Bridget, Micheal and Jax; Laila; Poppy and Scott; Dane; Samara, Indy and Aiyana; Mish, Mark, Max and Milly; Gemma; Jo.

Professional peeps who give me ongoing support (who are also my friends): Jeremy Worstman and the other JW lovelies; David Lopes from Gingko press; Sonia Le and Justine Clarke; Shinjiro Nishino and everyone at GAS Japan; *Frankie* magazine; *Inside Out* magazine; Lucy Feagins and Lisa Marie Corso from The Design Files; Shareen Joel at Share Design; Allana Coppel; Adam Rogers; Harvest Workroom; Megan Morton; Semi Permenant; Etsy; Doan from Loom; Mandy, Michael and Pheobe Munro; Right Angle; Paul McNeil and the Art Park.

Hardie Grant: Paul McNally – good one for trusting me to do this all over again! My two lovely and tolerant editors Lucy Heaver and Hannah Koelmeyer. Also Heather Menzies for your great expertise.

Kylie and Lluis for helping me to get the props to and from Butterland.

Kat Mew for helping me find chairs.

Last but not least: all the people who I don't know but have written me nice emails or commented on my blog and Instagram or introduced themselves to me – friendly and kind strangers are the best!

Published in 2013 by Hardie Grant Books

Hardie Grant Books (Australia)
Building 1, 658 Church Street
Richmond, Victoria 3121
www.hardiegrant.com.au

Hardie Grant Books (UK)
Second Floor, North Suite
Dudley House
Southampton Street
London WC2E 7HF
www.hardiegrant.co.uk

ISBN: 9781742706351

A Cataloguing-in-Publication entry is available from the catalogue of the National Library of Australia at www.nla.gov.au

Publishing Director: Paul McNally
Managing Editors: Lucy Heaver & Hannah Koelmeyer
Editor: Melody Lord
Design Manager: Heather Menzies
Designer: Michelle Mackintosh
Photography: Chris Middleton
Production Manager: Todd Rechner

Colour reproduction by Splitting Image Colour Studio
Printed in China by 1010 Printing International Limited

The publisher and Beci would like to thank Yellow Owl Workshop, After, Pan After, 5 Boroughs, Know Your Product, Loom Rugs, Cottage Industry, Mr Kitly, Ganim Store, Angelucci 20th Century, Third Drawer Down, i'm-home.com, Gleaners Inc, Cibi, Greg Hatton and Katie Marx Flowers for their generosity in supplying props for this book.

The publisher and Beci would like to thank helpers at the photoshoot: Alice Oehr, Amelia Leuzzi, Nat Turnbull, Stephanie Charters, Evie Smith, Claire Dilworth, Lucy Oehr, Andrea Shaw, Kirsty Davey, Kate Ulman, Indi Eisner, Chanie Stock and Ponie Curtis.

Models: Stephanie Charters, Tyke and Ari
Animal Models: Lulu, Tio, Otto and Brontë

Every effort has been made to incorporate correct information. The publishers regret any errors or omissions and invite readers to contribute up-to-date information to Hardie Grant Books.